University Cornell

Statutes of Cornell University

Adopted by the Executive committee May 19th, 1891

University Cornell

Statutes of Cornell University
Adopted by the Executive committee May 19th, 1891

ISBN/EAN: 9783337281694

Printed in Europe, USA, Canada, Australia, Japan

Cover: Foto ©Andreas Hilbeck / pixelio.de

More available books at **www.hansebooks.com**

STATUTES

OF

Cornell University

ADOPTED BY THE EXECUTIVE COMMITTEE MAY 19th, 1891,
IN ACCORDANCE WITH THE AUTHORITY OF THE
BOARD OF TRUSTEES CONFERRED
OCTOBER 30th, 1890.

———

PUBLISHED BY ORDER OF THE EXECUTIVE COMMITTEE,
CORNELL UNIVERSITY,
MAY, 1891.

CONTENTS.

I.	The Board of Trustees,	5
II.	The Executive Committee,	7
III.	The President,	8
IV.	The Treasurer,	9
V.	The Superintendent,	12
VI.	The University Senate,	14
VII.	The General Faculty,	14
VIII.	The College of Agriculture,	16
IX.	Sibley College,	18
X.	The College of Civil Engineering,	19
XI.	The School of Law,	20
XII.	The Susan Linn Sage College of Philosophy,	21
XIII.	Sage College,	21
XIV.	The University Library,	23
XV.	Fellowships,	25
XVI.	Scholarships,	27
XVII.	Miscellaneous Provisions,	28

STATUTES.

I.—THE BOARD OF TRUSTEES.

1. Subject to the Charter of the University and the laws of the State, the Board of Trustees has supreme control over the University, including each and every department, its property, conduct, and employés.

2. The officers of the Board shall be a Chairman, a Secretary, and a Treasurer. The Chairman shall be elected for the term for which he was chosen as a Trustee. The Secretary and Treasurer shall be elected according to the pleasure of the Board. The Secretary shall keep a record of the proceedings and have the same printed for the use of the members of the Board.

3. For the election of Trustees, ten members constitute a quorum, of whom eight votes shall be necessary to elect; for the transaction of other business eight members constitute a quorum.

4. There shall be three regular meetings of the Board in each year: one in Commencement week; one at a time to be fixed by the Executive Committee in the Winter, and one to be fixed by the same Committee in the Autumn. Notice of the Autumn and Winter meetings must be given by the Secretary thirty days in advance of the date fixed upon. Special meetings of the Board may be called by the Chairman, or by the Secretary, on the written request of five Trustees.

5. The President, all full Professors, Acting Professors, and Associate Professors must be elected by the full Board.

6. The financial and material interests of the University are under the immediate direction and care of the following Committees, the members of each to hold office until their successors are appointed: The Finance Committee; the Land Committee; the Committee on Plans of Campus and of Buildings; the Committee on Buildings and Grounds; the Committee on Appropriations; and the Auditing Committee.

7. The Finance Committee, in the absence of specific directions, has full power and authority to invest all funds of the University in such manner, at such places, and upon such securities as it shall deem

best, and it shall report the investments so made from time to time to the Board of Trustees or the Executive Committee.

8. The Land Committee, in the absence of specific directions, has all power and authority to make sales of lands and timber, to decide all questions relating thereto or arising therefrom, and to exercise such care, custody, and control, over such lands as may be necessary.

9. The Committee on Plans of Campus and of Buildings shall have charge of the procuring and submitting to the Trustees or Executive Committee of plans for any extension or modification of the University's landed property, for roads through it, and for structures upon it. The said Committee shall consist of the Chairman of the Board of Trustees, the President of the University, and three other Trustees to be elected by the Board, or in absence of action by the full Board, by the Executive Committee.

10. The Committees on Buildings and Grounds shall have general charge of the Real Property belonging to the University in Ithaca. It is made the duty of this Committee to report to the Executive Committee and the Board of Trustees from time to time in regard to the condition of the property under its charge, and to make such recommendations as may seem to be demanded by the welfare of the University.

11. The Committee on Appropriations shall consider all recommendations made by the several heads of departments in their annual reports; and, after comparing the sum of the amounts called for with the estimated income for the following year, shall recommend in a Report to the Board at the October meeting, such appropriations as they may deem for the best interests of the University.

12. The Auditing Committee shall make a careful examination of all the accounts of the Treasurer; shall compare the amount of fees received from students with the list of students in the University; shall compare the amount of securities and money in the possession of the University with the amounts indicated in the Treasurer's Report; and in general shall satisfy itself by proper scrutiny that the Annual Report of the Treasurer is correct as a whole and in detail. For this purpose the Committee is authorized to employ the services of an expert bookkeeper at the expense of the University.

13. To the inventory of the available assets of the University, contained on page 4 of the Treasurer's report for the year 1889–90, amounting in all to $4,678,729.77, any additions to the general fund which shall hereafter be received from sales of land, gifts, or bequests in cash or productive securities or property, shall be added, and entered upon the Treasurer's books as the income producing cap-

ital of the University ; and hereafter there shall be no appropriation, use, or expenditure of said principal except in case of insufficiency of sales of lands to pay taxes and expenses of carrying the same, and except it be to meet an extraordinary emergency, and in the latter case only upon a vote of a majority of all the members of the Board of Trustees. But nothing in this provision shall invalidate the loan from said fund of the sum yet due on the appropriation of $80,000 by the Board for the Chemical Laboratory.

14. Whenever the Board shall receive from the President a nomination for a professorship in accordance with the method hereinafter provided, the Board shall proceed to confirm or reject such nomination ; but such confirmation or rejection shall be by ballot, said ballot to be not by a single open vote to be cast by any one person, but by the ballots of all present and voting.

15. The expenses incurred by non-resident Trustees in attending meetings of the Board shall be audited and paid by the Treasurer.

II.—THE EXECUTIVE COMMITTEE.

1. The Trustees residing in Ithaca and such other Trustees as may at the time of a meeting be in Ithaca constitute the Executive Committee. The officers of the Executive Committee shall be a Chairman and a Secretary who shall hold office until their successors are appointed. The Executive Committee may exercise all the power of the Board of Trustees not inconsistent with the acts and resolutions of the Board, subject, however, to reversal or modification of its action by the full Board. Five shall be a quorum. It may, when necessary, elect Assistant Professors, Instructors, and non-resident lecturers, and any other needed officers or employés, except those whose election is restricted to the full Board. Assistant Professors shall be elected for three years, and may be re-elected after that period by a two-thirds vote of the entire Committee. Instructors shall be elected for one year. After three years of service they may be re-elected by a two-thirds vote of the entire Committee.

2. It is the duty of the Chairman to exercise the ordinary functions of a presiding officer.

3. It is the duty of the Secretary to keep a record of the proceedings of the Committee, to have the record printed and sent to each member of the Board of Trustees.

4. For the more intelligent supervision of the several departments of the University, the Executive Committee has appointed the following Standing Committees, the members of each of which shall hold office till their successors are appointed.

(1). The Committee on the departments of Mathematics and Applied Sciences : Trustees Williams, Lord, and H. W. Sage.

(2). The Committee on the departments and museums of Natural History : Trustees Van Cleef, Boardman, and Tyler.

(3). The Committee on Ancient and Modern Languages : Trustees Tyler, Lord, and Van Cleef.

(4). The Committee on the Schools of History and Political Science, and Philosophy : Trustees White, Adams, and Lord.

(5). The Committee on Sage College : Trustees H. W. Sage. Adams, and the Treasurer.

(6). The Committee on Physical Culture and Military Tactics : Trustess W. H. Sage, Van Cleef, and Williams.

III.—THE PRESIDENT.

1. The President is the head of the educational departments of the University, and of each of them.

2. In the absence of special provisions, he is the medium of communication between the Trustees and the officers of instruction, the Faculties, and the Senate.

3. Before action affecting any department, he shall consult with the professors thereof in respect to the necessities of such department and the best modes of supplying the same. It shall be his duty to determine, with the approval of the Executive Committee, the appropriate duties and labors of all officers of instruction; to nominate to the Senate for appointment, as hereinafter provided, all full professors; to nominate all other officers of instruction ; to see that all officers of instruction are doing a proper amount and satisfactory quality of work ; to provide that lecture and recitation rooms are as much and as economically used as successful work will permit ; to aid, so far as he may, in keeping the expenses of the University within its income ; and, subject to other regulations made or to be made, to watch over and care for the buildings, apparatus, libraries, and other property ; and in all ways by his reports and conduct to seek to protect the property and promote the welfare of the University.

4. Whenever any full professorship is to be filled, the President of the University shall, upon the request of the Board of Trustees or of the Executive Committee, seek diligently and to the best of his ability, and, bearing in mind the provision of the fundamental charter of the University, which forbids him to take cognizance of any political or religious views which any candidate may or may not hold, shall

nominate to the Senate the person whom he may consider most worthy to occupy the vacancy to be filled.

5. The President shall prepare an Annual Report on the condition and needs of the University, shall cause the same to be printed, and shall send a copy to each member of the Board prior to its meeting in October of each year.

6. The President and the Dean of the General Faculty shall have supervision of the official publications of the University.

7. The traveling expenses of the President incurred at the request of the Trustees, or for the business and welfare of the University, shall be audited and paid by the Treasurer.

IV.—THE TREASURER.

1. The Treasurer shall make purchases for the various departments upon the requisition of the Professors in charge to the amount of the appropriations made to their respective departments.

2. Any excess of expenditure by any Professor beyond the amount apportioned for the use of his department, if the same shall be recognized and paid by the University, shall be charged to said Professor personally and shall remain a charge against him, to be retained out of his salary, until such time as the appropriation applicable to the payment thereof shall be sufficient to pay the same, when it shall be credited to such Professor and charged to such appropriation.

3. No purchases shall be made or indebtedness created in the name of the University except upon the order of the Treasurer.

4. The salaries of all officers of instruction shall be paid in nine equal monthly installments beginning October 15th and ending June 15th, and the salaries of the Treasurer, clerks, and other salaried employés shall be paid monthly on the 1st day of each month.

5. Any student failing to settle his account with the Treasurer within ten days after the opening of each term, shall, upon the recommendation of the Treasurer, be dropped from the University, but such student, in the discretion of the President, may be restored upon payment of his account and producing the Treasurer's receipt therefor.

6. The tuition fee of any student who is called away from the University within ten days after registration day, may be refunded on just cause shown.

7. From and after August 1st, 1891, the annual tuition fee for students not exempt therefrom, shall be, in the School of Law, in the Medical Preparatory course, and in the courses in Arts, Philosophy, Letters, and Science, $100, $40 to be paid at the beginning of the first.

term, $35 at the beginning of the second term, and $25 at the beginning of the third term ; in all other courses, including Optional and Special students, it shall be $125, $50 to be paid at the beginning of the first term, $40 at the beginning of the second, and $35 at the beginning of the third.

8. Each person receiving a first degree from the University shall pay therefor a fee of five dollars ; and each person receiving an advanced degree shall pay therefor a fee of ten dollars.

9. Such graduation fee shall be collected by the Treasurer at least ten days before Commencement, and the Treasurer shall furnish to the Secretary of the Faculty a list of persons who have paid such fees at least one week before Commencement.

10. In the Summer Course of Entomology tuition is free for all graduate students that are candidates for an advanced degree, and to all students matriculated in any of the regular classes of the University. All other students shall pay to the Treasurer within ten days after the opening of the school the sum of $25.00 for tuition.

11. Students working in the shops or laboratories of Sibley College shall pay within ten days after each term begins the sum of $5.00 each for materials used.

12. Students using the laboratories in Natural History, Chemistry, Physics, and Civil Engineering, shall pay the entire expenses of supplies consumed in the process of investigation or instruction. A suitable amount to be certified by the professor in charge of those departments shall be deposited with the Treasurer by each of such students at the beginning of each term as a guaranty fund.

13. Graduate students are exempted from payment of annual tuition fees when they have been duly admitted by the proper authorities as candidates for an advanced degree and are regularly pursuing the courses of study leading to such degrees in accordance with the prescribed requirements of the proper faculty.

14. Students pursuing full courses in Agriculture, and special students in Agriculture, are exempt from tuition fees, but they shall not change such course for any other course without first paying the regular tuition fees for all the time spent in the Agricultural course prior to such change. This section shall be inoperative after the completion of the Agricultural building provided for at the meeting of the Board of Trustees in October, 1890.

15. To enable the Treasurer to make up his accounts against students for payment at the beginning of each term it shall be the duty of the Registrar to furnish him with a list of all students registered, as soon as practicable after the opening of each term. For the same

purpose the professors of Natural History, Physics, Chemistry, Civil Engineering, and Mechanic Arts shall furnish the Treasurer with a list of the students in the laboratories of each of those departments as early as practicable, with the amount which each student is required to pay or deposit as hereinbefore provided. And any student failing to make such payment or deposit to the satisfaction of the Treasurer within ten days after the beginning of the term shall be excluded from his classes or shops by the Professor in charge.

16. The Treasurer is the custodian of the corporate seal; and he is authorized and it shall be his duty to execute in the name of Cornell University all deeds, contracts, and other instruments in writing requisite or necessary to be executed except that where for any reason such instrument must be signed by the President, Chairman, or Secretary of the Board of Trustees, such officers or any of them may execute the same in like manner. But in all matters pertaining to degrees conferred by the University, the seal shall be under the direction of the President.

17. And the said officers are authorized collectively and individually under the corporate seal to execute any release or satisfaction of any security upon payment of the same, and any deed of real estate sold by the Board of Trustees, the Executive Committee, or the Land Committee, or any other instrument in writing required to be executed by the authority of the University aforesaid, and wherever requisite or necessary to affix the corporate seal to said deeds or other written instruments.

18. All investments of University funds shall be regarded as made for the University as a whole and not for any specific fund; and the annual income arising from such investments shall be distributed *pro rata* among the several specific funds held by and being the absolute property of the University. But such funds as by their holding are or may be subject to specific conditions requiring the principal and interest to be kept separate from other funds shall not be subject to the above rule.

19. The Treasurer shall set apart each year five per cent. of the annual income of the University, (not however including the income derived directly from the United States), to cover such losses as may occur through bad investments, fire, or otherwise.

20. The sum so set apart shall be invested like other permanent funds of the University and shall be a source of reliance or guaranty fund to replace any extraordinary losses in the future.

21. The Treasurer shall make his annual report to the Board of Trustees at the first regular meeting after the first day of August in

each year. The Treasurer shall print and send to each Trustee a copy of such report so far as may be necessary, and so far as shall be approved by the Finance Committee.

22. The Treasurer is authorized by the Board of Trustees to receipt in the name of the University for all funds received from the United States or the State of New York for the Agricultural Experiment Station and for the departments of Agriculture and the Mechanic Arts.

23. Until further action a bond shall be given by the Treasurer to the amount of $25,000.

V.—THE SUPERINTENDENT.

1. The Superintendent shall have control of all the buildings, grounds, roads, bridges, sidewalks, reservoir, steam, water, gas, and sewer pipes, and all other out-of-door property on or about the campus and belonging to the University ; and shall make, or cause to be made all necessary repairs, work, or changes to fit the property for its uses. It is understood that the grounds set apart for the farm, the Department of Horticulture, and the Agricultural Experiment Station, are exempt from this superintendence. But no extraordinary expenses, labor, or changes shall be made, except upon the order of the trustees, and no expenses of any kind shall be incurred or purchase made except upon the order of the Treasurer.

2. Upon request of the Trustees or of the Executive Committee, it shall be his duty to examine and report upon the plans and specifications of all new buildings to be erected upon the campus, and upon like request to superintend their construction.

3. He shall have the charge of all janitors employed, and shall see that they faithfully perform their duties ; shall recommend the dismissal of any janitor whenever the conduct and services of such janitor are unsatisfactory ; shall require them to practice, and shall enforce a proper economy in the use of steam, heat, and water so that neither be wasted.

4. He shall have charge of all fire apparatus in and about the buildings and grounds, shall make suitable rules, regulations, and organization for its prompt and efficient use and shall be held responsible for its condition and fitness for use at all times ; shall by frequent inspection and careful examination take extreme precaution against accidental fires, and in the event of fire shall have control of all the means for its extinguishment. He shall, from time to time, examine and report on the subject of fire escapes in all University buildings occupied by

students, and shall see that such fire escapes as have been authorized, are put in place and maintained, as far as possible, in a state of efficiency.

5. He shall direct and have control of the night watchmen, and shall file each day the records of trips for the previous night with the Treasurer.

6. He shall prevent as far as possible all trespasses upon the grounds or in or about the buildings, shall maintain suitable notices, and, if necessary, put up gates to warn people that the roads, lawns, shrubbery, and flowers are private property ; shall, as far as possible, forbid and prevent any person or persons from allowing horses, cows, sheep, or other animals to run at large on the University grounds, or to be attached to or do injury to any trees or shrubbery; shall not permit any employé not a teacher to render any service for others than the University during the hours or time for which service is due the University ; shall forbid and prevent all employés from using or disposing of any materials or property belonging to the University except for University purposes ; shall, as far as possible, forbid and prevent any and every person from marring, defacing, or injuring any of the buildings or property of the University, and from posting, writing, chalking, or painting any notice or other communication or thing upon any of the buildings, or upon any doors, windows, walls, or stairways of the buildings, or sidewalks ; shall report any person or persons violating this ordinance, or committing any trespass or nuisance upon the grounds, to the President.

7. The Superintendent may give permits to any persons entitled thereto to dig ditches, make connections with sewer, gas, or water-pipes, or otherwise break up the soil on the campus, upon the written agreement of a person receiving such permit to restore the ground to its former state and condition, and to pay any damage which the University may sustain, or be put to by reason of such digging of the grounds.

8. The Superintendent shall have no charge or control over the Sage College Conservatory or over any landscape gardening, ornamentation or decoration of the grounds, plans for grading, terracing, or otherwise laying out or improving the campus unless by special order of the Trustees, or Executive Committee. Each and all of the matters aforesaid shall be under the supervision and management of the Professor of Botany, until otherwise ordered.

VI.—THE UNIVERSITY SENATE.

1. The University Senate shall consist of the President of the University and all the full Professors.

2. It shall be the duty of the Senate to counsel and advise in regard to all nominations for professorships; to consider and make recommendations in regard to such courses of study as may pertain to more than one Faculty of the University; and, in general, to consider and make recommendations upon any questions of University policy that may be submitted to this body by the Trustees, or the President, or either of the Faculties.

3. Whenever the University Senate shall receive from the President a nomination for a professorship in accordance with the method hereinbefore provided, the Senate, after proper deliberation, shall vote by ballot, yea or nay, upon the nomination, and this action, with any reasons for it which the Senate may see fit to submit, shall be certified to the Board of Trustees.

4. The meetings of the Senate may be called by the President, or by the Secretary upon the written application of any five members; and at such meetings the President, or in his absence the Dean of the General Faculty shall preside. The Senate shall have a secretary whose duty it shall be to keep a record of proceedings, and call all meetings under the direction of the proper authority.

VII.—THE GENERAL FACULTY.

1. The General Faculty of the University shall consist of the President, of a Dean, and of such Professors, Acting Professors, Associate Professors, and Assistant Professors, as have been or shall hereafter be appointed to departments under its jurisdiction.

2. The President of the University, whenever present, shall be the presiding officer of the Faculty; shall have the right of a deciding vote in case of a tie; shall appoint all committees provided for by the Faculty unless otherwise ordered; and shall call extra meetings of the Faculty whenever in his judgment such meetings may be called for by the welfare of the University.

3. The Dean of the General Faculty shall be appointed by the Trustees on the nomination of the President and with the concurrence of the Faculty. It shall be his duty to preside at Faculty meetings in the absence of the President; to receive and act upon such applications of students as may be referred to him by the Faculty; to prepare and conduct the business of the several committees of which he may be made by the Faculty *ex officio* chairman; and in general, except as otherwise provided, to act as the executive officer of the Faculty.

4. The Faculty has power to determine the requirements for admission to such departments of the University as are under its jurisdiction ; to prescribe and define the various courses of study for undergraduate and graduate students ; to determine, subject to revision by the Trustees, the requirements for such degrees as are offered to students under its jurisdiction ; to enact and enforce such rules for the guidance of its own students as it may deem best adapted to the interests of the University ; to fill all University Fellowships and Scholarships in accordance with the provisions therefor made by the Trustees; to make rules for its own methods of procedure ; to delegate any of its powers and duties to any of the Special Faculties for final action or decision ; to recommend to the Trustees such candidates for degrees as may have completed the requirements ; and in general, to exercise the customary duties of college faculties.

5. It is the duty of the Faculty, through its Secretary, to certify to the Treasurer the filling of all Fellowships and University Scholarships immediately after such action has been taken.

6. The Faculty must not recommend any applicant for graduation, until graduating fees and all dues to the University have been paid, or satisfactorily arranged ; nor shall the Faculty grant any application for leave of absence unless such application is endorsed by the Treasurer, certifying that all dues have been paid or satisfactorily arranged. In order that there may be no delay, it is required that all candidates for graduation must pay or satisfactorily arrange all dues, including graduating fees, at least ten days before commencement; but in case of failure to graduate, the graduating fee will be returned.

7. The Faculty shall keep a complete record of its proceedings, and its general legislation may be printed at the expense of the University.

8. All officers of instruction are expected to be present for duty at the University from the beginning of each term to the close of the examinations; and at the end of the year, till the close of Commencement day. Applications for absence of not more than seven days should be made to the President, of more than seven days to the Executive Committee. No officer of instruction shall engage in any other occupation which shall interfere with or impair the particular discharge of his duties in the University.

9. The heads of the different departments of instruction, shall each, before the first day of July in each year, furnish to the Treasurer, a full and true inventory of the personal property belonging to the University in their departments or under their control ; together with a list of all articles presented to the University during the year for the use of their departments with the value of the same and the names of the donors.

10. No person shall be allowed to borrow or take away from their particular places in the University buildings, or their particular use on the University grounds any philosophical, or other illustrative apparatus, maps, charts, diagrams, or specimens from any cabinet or museum, without an order from the Professor responsible therefor, or in his absence, an order in writing signed by the President or the Treasurer.

11. Every Assistant Professor or Instructor shall act as examiner upon the written request of the head of his department, countersigned by the President.

12. Whenever any Professor, Acting Professor, Associate Professor, or Assistant Professor has continuously served the University for at least seven years, he may, subject to the approval of the Executive Committee, have leave of absence for not more than one year, upon the following limitations and conditions :

(a.) During such leave of absence one-half of the salary attached to the position held by the applicant is to be paid.

(b.) Application for such absence must be made through the President on or before January 1st preceding the collegiate year during which absence is desired.

(c.) No more than one absence from any department of instruction will be granted in any one year ; and where more than one application from any department is made, precedence will be given in the order of seniority of service.

(d.) Whenever for any reason the Trustees shall think that such absence will be injurious to the best interests of the University, they reserve the right to withhold such leave of absence.

(e.) Arrangements for continuing the work of instruction in case of such application must be made without expense to the University beyond the full salary of the absentee.

13. In any Faculty of the University the final question as to the suspension, dismissal, or expulsion of a student or body of students, whether graduate or undergraduate, shall be decided by the ballots of those present who are entitled to vote upon the question ; each person thus entitled to vote casting one ballot. The power to cast a single ballot in behalf of the said Faculty, or of a majority of the same, shall never, in any such question of suspension, dismissal, or expulsion of a student, be delegated to any one person, or to any committee.

VIII.—THE COLLEGE OF AGRICULTURE.

1. The College of Agriculture consists of such departments of the University as are brought into organic relations for the purpose of furnishing facilities for didactic and experimental work in the

several branches connected with instruction in Agriculture and with the Agricultural Experiment Station.

2. The College is thus constituted by the co-ordination of the departments of General, Analytical, and Agricultural Chemistry, Botany, Horticulture, Vertebrate and Invertebrate Zoology and Entomology, Veterinary Science, Geology, and the several branches of Theoretical and Practical Agriculture. The officers of these several departments constitute the Faculty of the College.

3. The Faculty of the College shall have general charge of the interests of Agricultural students, shall consider such modifications of the courses of study as may be duly placed before them, and shall make such recommendations to the General Faculty as may seem to them conducive to the interests of the College. All students of the College are amenable to the General Faculty.

4. The Professor of Agriculture is the Director of the College. It is his duty to preside at all meetings of the Faculty in the absence of the President, to promote in all practicable ways the welfare of the College, to prepare or cause to be prepared all necessary announcements, and to make an Annual Report to the President on the condition and needs of the College.

5. The Professor of Agriculture shall have under his control and management the University farm and all the farm buildings; shall employ and discharge at his discretion all common laborers employed in the cultivation and care of the crops and stock on the farm; shall purchase such stock, seed, or materials as may be provided for by appropriations for such purposes, at his discretion, and also sell, or otherwise dispose of the same; shall make out, present, and collect all accounts and bills accruing from the sale of productions of the University farm; shall pay monthly into the University treasury all sums received for such sales, accompanied by an itemized statement of the sources of such receipts; and shall make an Annual Report of the products and condition of the farm to the President of the University.

6. The Professor of Horticulture shall have under his control and management such grounds as have been, or may from time to time be set apart by the Trustees for the purposes of Horticulture. The employment and direction of subordinates, the purchase of materials, and the disposition of products of the department are under the same general regulations as those of the department of Agriculture.

7. For the purpose of giving definiteness and unity to the work of the Agricultural Experiment Station, there is established a board of control, known as the Agricultural Experiment Station Council. This Council consists of the President of the University, of two other members of the Board of Trustees, one of whom is the President of

the State Agricultural Society, and one of whom is elected from the Trustees residing in Ithaca, together with the Director of the Experiment Station, and the heads of those departments in which the work of the Station is done, viz.: the Professor of Agriculture, the Professor of Agricultural Chemistry, the Professor of Veterinary Science, the Professor of Botany, the Assistant Professor of Cryptogamic Botany, the Professor of Entomology, and the Professor of Practical and Experimental Horticulture.

8. It is the duty of this Council to recommend to the Trustees the apportionment of the work to be done at the Experiment Station by the various departments and the proper appropriations for the same; to make any other recommendations they may think conducive to the efficiency of the Station, and, in general, to have such management of the affairs of the Station as may be assigned to them by the Trustees.

9. The duties of the Director of the Experiment Station are to carry out the measures determined upon by the Trustees and the Council; to publish and distribute the bulletins of the Station as required by law; to prepare an Annual Report to the President of the work of the year; and, in general, to act as the chief executive officer of the Station.

10. The Director shall certify to all bills against the Station, and such bills when duly certified, shall be paid by the Treasurer out of the funds belonging thereto.

11. No purchases shall be made, or expenses incurred, on account of the Agricultural Experiment Station, except through the office and by the authority of the Director, and all bills for such purchases shall be made out in every case against the Agricultural Experiment Station of Cornell University.

12. It is considered the duty of every professor connected with the Experiment Station to contribute directly to the experiments carried on by such Station, and to the preparation of their results for publication.

13. The Director of the Agricultural Experiment Station is authorized to draw against the credit given to the Station for materials sold by the Station and deposited with the Treasurer.

IX.—SIBLEY COLLEGE.

1. This College embraces the departments of Mechanical Engineering, Electrical Engineering, Mechanic Arts, Industrial Drawing and Art, and all the appliances for Heat, Light, Water, and Power.

2. The College is placed by the Trustees in the special charge of a

Director who shall have control of the whole workings of the College, shall recommend to the President all persons for appointment as professors, assistant professors, instructors, foremen, engineers, and other employés in the college and be responsible for their efficiency ; shall be the custodian of the buildings, tools, machinery, models, apparatus, and other property and chattels of the College ; shall be responsible for their proper use and preservation, and for the efficiency of the motive power and the power for furnishing light and heat ; shall control and direct the instruction of students, and the labor of the employés ; and within the means placed at his disposal, shall do all he can to promote the prosperity of the College and University. He shall make an annual report to the President on the condition and needs of the College, and from time to time shall make such other reports and recommendations as may seem to be called for.

3. The University will supply Sibley College with such instruction as may be needed in mathematics, chemistry, physics, including elementary electricity and electrical measurements, modern languages and other extra-professional studies. Arrangements for such supply shall be made by the General Faculty on the request of the Sibley College authorities.

4. The department of Heat, Light, and Water, and all the materials and equipment therefor except those in charge of the Superintendent, shall be in charge of the Director, who shall appoint from the Faculty of Sibley College, or from its employes, fit and proper persons to take charge of and manage the same ; and the persons so appointed shall be held responsible by the Director for the condition of the tools, machinery, and property, and for their efficiency at all times to accomplish the work and purposes for which they were intended.

X.—THE COLLEGE OF CIVIL ENGINEERING.

1. This college consists of such branches of the University as are brought into organic relations for the purpose of affording facilities for thorough and comprehensive studies in Civil Engineering.

2. The branches represented in this organization are Bridge Engineering, Railroad Engineering, Sanitary and Municipal Engineering, Hydraulic Engineering, and Geodetic Engineering.

3. The college is placed by the Trustees in the special charge of a Director, who, subject to such rules as from time to time may be made by the Trustees, shall have control of the workings of the college ; shall recommend to the President all persons for appointment in the several grades of instruction, and be responsible for their efficiency ;

shall have charge of such portions of Lincoln Hall as have been or may hereafter be assigned to the use of the college by the Trustees; shall be the custodian of the tools, machinery, models, apparatus, drawings, and other property of the college; shall be responsible for their proper use and preservation; shall control and direct the instruction of students and the labor of employés; and, within the means placed at his disposal, shall do all he can to promote the prosperity of the college and the University. He shall make an annual report to the President, and from time to time shall make such other reports and recommendations as may seem to be called for by the condition and needs of the college.

4. The University will supply this college with such instruction as may be needed in mathematics, chemistry, physics, modern languages, and other extra-professional studies. Arrangements for such supply are to be made by the General Faculty at the request of the director.

XI.—THE SCHOOL OF LAW.

1. The Faculty of the School of Law consists of the President of the University, of a Dean, of a Secretary, and of such Professors as may from time to time be elected thereto by the Trustees. It shall be the duty of the Faculty to fix upon the terms of admission to the School; to provide for such courses of study as it may deem practicable and desirable; subject to revision by the Trustees; to fix upon the conditions of graduation; to conduct all examinations; to nominate to the Trustees non-resident lecturers; and to frame such rules and administer such discipline as it may deem necessary for the welfare of the School.

2. It shall be the duty of the Dean to preside at Faculty meetings in the absence of the President; to promote in all practicable ways the general welfare of the School; and to make or cause to be made an Annual Report to the President on the condition and needs of the School.

3. It shall be the duty of the Secretary under the direction of the Dean or of the Faculty to prepare and publish the announcements of the School; to keep a record of Faculty meetings; to conduct the necessary correspondence with non-resident lecturers and with applicants for admission; to make out all necessary schedules of exercises and examinations; and to prepare statements in regard to the School to be published in the Annual Register of the University.

4. Students of the School of Law are required to register in the office of the Registrar of the General Faculty, but, after registration, they are amenable only to the Faculty of the School of Law.

XII.—THE SUSAN LINN SAGE SCHOOL OF PHILOSOPHY.

1. This School, established Oct. 22, 1890, in accordance with the terms of an endowment provided by the Hon. Henry W. Sage, consists of the several departments of instruction that are brought into organic relations for the purpose of affording facilities for generous and comprehensive studies in Philosophy and Ethics.

2. The departments thus brought into organic relations are Ancient Philosophy, Modern Philosophy, Psychology, Logic, Pedagogy, The History and Philosophy of Religion and of Christian Ethics, and such other departments as may, from time to time, be added by the Trustees. The officers of instruction in these departments shall constitute the Faculty of the School.

3. The school is placed by the Trustees under the direction of a Dean, who shall have general superintendence of the workings of the School; shall preside at all meetings of the Faculty in the absence of the President; shall recommend to the President all persons for appointment in the several grades of instruction, and be responsible for their efficiency; shall within the means placed at his disposal do all that he can to promote the prosperity of the School and the University; shall make an Annual Report to the President, and from time to time shall make such other reports and recommendations as may seem to be called for by the condition and needs of the School.

XIII.—SAGE COLLEGE.

1. Subject to the rules and directions of the Trustees, Sage College is under the management of the Principal and the Business Manager.

2. It is the duty of the Principal to administer the rules adopted by the Trustees for the guidance of students residing in Sage College; to have the general charge of the social interests of the students of Sage College; to advise them in regard to all matters of health and conduct; to determine the use of the Sage College reception room, subject to such regulations as are hereinafter provided; to report to the President of the University any such infractions of the rules as she may deem it necessary to call to his attention; and to make an Annual Report to the President in regard to the work of the year, and in regard to any changes which she may deem advisable.

3. It is the duty of the Business Manager to have the care of the Sage College building in all its parts, except those which have been assigned to the care of the department of Botany; to keep the public

and private rooms of the building in good order; to pay special attention to the sanitary condition of the building; to furnish all supplies for the table in proper variety, quantity, and quality; to provide that the building throughout be kept neat and attractive in appearance; to close the building and extinguish the lights in the public rooms at 10 p. m., except in those special cases that are duly provided for; to take every reasonable precaution against fire; to make out and collect all proper bills against students and boarders within the College; to employ and pay all necessary service; to make such uniform charges for the unusual use of the reception room and other rooms as may be agreed upon at the beginning of each year, in consultation with the Treasurer of the University and the Principal of Sage College; to make an Annual Report to the Treasurer at the end of each college year; and, in general, in accordance with the terms of his contract with the Trustees of the University, to have charge of all the material interests of the College.

4. All women admitted to the University as students are required to room and board at Sage College unless excused for due cause by the Sage College Committee.

5. All students residing in Sage College are required to be in the College building at 10 o'clock at night; and, except in case of some general entertainment in the building, are required to be in their own private rooms. The only exception to this requirement permitted will be in case of absence from the building with the Principal or with her permission secured in advance.

6. Quiet must be observed in the corridors and private rooms after 10 o'clock at night.

7. Every student is required, on going out in the evening, to leave her name with the Principal, and to state where and with whom she is going. If the Principal is not in her room, written notice must be left on the table inside the door of her room.

8. Calls from young gentlemen may be received in the reception room on two specified evenings in the week, from 7.30 to 9.30 o'clock, the evenings to be designated by the Principal after due consultation of the convenience of the young ladies. At all other times the cards of young gentlemen calling will be delivered by the porter to the Principal, and will then be forwarded only in case of special necessity.

9. All students residing in Sage College are expected to assemble in the reception room each day immediately after tea for such announcements as the Principal may desire to make. This requirement may be waived at the discretion of the Principal.

10. On all questions of propriety on the part of students residing in

Sage College, the Principal is recognized by the Trustees as the authoritative judge. In case of any violation of either of the rules, or of the requirements of the Principal in the matter of conduct, or of any persistent misdemeanor of any kind, the Principal is expected to report the case to the President of the University.

XIV.—THE UNIVERSITY LIBRARY.

1. The general care and supervision of the University Library is entrusted to a Library Council. This council consists of the President of the University, who shall be *ex-officio* Chairman of the Council, the Librarian, or, in his absence, the Acting Librarian, and five elected members, one of whom shall be elected by the Executive Committee and four by the General Faculty. The election of members shall take place annually as near the beginning of the collegiate year as may be practicable. Persons elected shall hold office till their successors are chosen.

2. For the election of members from the Faculty that body shall be divided into two groups, and each group at the first election after the adoption of this statute shall elect two members, one of whom shall hold office for one year and one for two years, the term of each being determined by lot. Each year thereafter one member shall be elected annually by each group for two years.

3. The two groups for the election of members shall be constituted as follows, viz.: 1. The Group of Science; 2. The Group of Letters. The Group of Science for the purposes of this act shall be deemed to include those members of the General Faculty who give instruction in the departments of Agriculture, Architecture, Civil Engineering, Mechanical and Electrical Engineering, Mathematics, Physics, Chemistry, Physical Culture, Military Tactics, and the several branches of Natural History. The group of Letters shall be deemed to include those members of the Faculty who give instruction in the departments of the several Languages, of History and Political Science, and of Philosophy and Ethics. In each of the groups the election shall be by ballot, and the result of the ballot shall be communicated to the Executive Committee by the Secretary of the Faculty. In case a member of the Faculty should be a member of both groups, he may choose the group in which he will act, and he may vote and be voted for in that group and not in the other.

4. It shall be the duty of the Library Council to apportion the book funds between the various departments of instruction as may best accord with the interests of the University, and to recom-

mend and submit to the Trustees for their approval all questions pertaining to the apportionment of the funds, binding, cataloguing, and in general, to all accommodations, arrangements, and rules for the administration of the Library. After the apportionment of the book funds each year shall have been approved by the Executive Committee, the Treasurer shall be authorized, unless otherwise instructed, to purchase books approved by the Council, not exceeding the amount of the appropriation ; but no subordinate shall be employed, salaries paid, or expenses of any kind incurred which shall not first have been approved by the Executive Committee, and after an appropriation duly made by them. All business of a financial character shall be transacted through the Treasurer of the University.

5. The duties of the Librarian shall be to take charge of the internal administration of the Library, and, with his subordinates, to keep it in complete working order for the use of Professors, students, and others entitled to it ; to conduct its correspondence ; to make an Annual Report to the President of its condition, and of all additions to it ; and to perform such other duties as may be imposed upon him from time to time by the Trustees.

6. The Librarian and President have power to approve orders, signed by the Professors at the head of the departments, for ordinary working books, but shall refer to the Council all orders for costly or otherwise exceptional books.

7. The selection and purchase, subject to the approval of the Library Council, of books in the fields of study to which the President White Library is specially devoted, is in accordance with the resolutions of the Trustees of the University on January 19, 1887, entrusted to a body consisting of the President of the University, *ex officio*, the Honorable Andrew Dickson White, the Librarian of the University, the Librarian of the President White Library, *ex officio*, and one representative to be chosen by the Library Council from the special faculty of History and Political Science.

8. The fields of study in which the selection and purchase of books for the President White Library may be made shall be interpreted to be : (1) General History and the sciences auxiliary to history (as geography, chronology, palæography, diplomatics, pneumismatics, archæology) ; (2) Ancient History, Oriental and European ; (3) Mediæval History, political, social, and ecclesiastical ; (4) Modern History of the Old World.

9. The two Fellows on the President White foundation, to wit, the Fellow in modern history and the Fellow in political and social science, shall give to the services of the President White Library, subject

to the direction of the librarian thereof, not less than four hours daily of personal attendance as an equivalent for the hours of teaching required under the regulations of the Faculty, save when, with the consent of the Librarian of the University, they are assigned to other duties by the special faculty of History and Political Science.

XV.—FELLOWSHIPS.

1. There have been established at this University four classes of Fellowships, as follows :

(a). Eight University Fellowships, denominated respectively, the Cornell Fellowship ; the McGraw Fellowship ; the Sage Fellowship ; the Schuyler Fellowship ; the Sibley Fellowship ; the Goldwin Smith Fellowship ; the President White Fellowship ; and the Erastus Brooks Fellowship.

(b). Two President White Fellowships, denominated ; first, the President White Fellowship of Modern History ; second, the President White Fellowship of Political and Social Science.

(c). Three Susan Linn Sage Fellowships in Philosophy and Ethics.

(d). Two Fellowships in Polttical Economy and Finance.

2. The President White Fellowships in History and Political and Social Science have an annual value of $500.00 each ; the others have an annual value of $400.00 each, the money being payable to the holders thereof in three equal parts, one part on the 15th of December, one on the 15th of March, and one on the 15th of June.

3. All candidates for Fellowships must be graduates of this University, or of some other institution having equivalent courses of instruction, and must be men or women of high character and marked ability in some important department of study.

4. Fellows will be selected by the General Faculty on the recommendation of the head of that department in which the applicant desires to carry on the principal part of his work.

5. All applications and testimonials must be filed with the Registrar on or before the 15th of May of the collegiate year preceding the one for which application is made.

6. The term of each Fellowship is one year ; but the term may be extended to two years, provided the extension does not increase the number of Fellows beyond that named in paragraph 1 of this act.

7. In view of the fact that practical University instruction will be of use in training said Fellows for future usefulness, each holder of a Fellowship shall be liable to render service to the University in the work of instruction or examinations to the extent of four hours per

week throughout the collegiate year. The distribution and assignment of this service in each individual case shall be determined by the head of the department in which the Fellow is doing his principal work. It is expected that the President White Fellows in History and Political Science will do a large part of their study in the President White Library, and, to this end, it is required, that, except when, with the consent of the Librarian of the University, they are excused or assigned to other duties by the Faculty of History and Political Science, said Fellows shall be in attendance in the Library not less than four hours each per day.

8. No person shall hold at one time more than one Fellowship, except in the case hereafter specified under paragraph 12 of this statute, and any Fellow may be dispossessed of the income of his Fellowship by action of the Faculty, if he shall be guilty of any offence, or if he shall continue in any course of conduct, which, in the opinion of the Faculty, shall render him unworthy of holding such Fellowship ; but the final action in such cases by the Faculty shall be by ballot, and shall require a two-thirds vote.

9. Vacancies in Fellowships that occur after October 1st, in order to be filled, shall require a three-fourths vote of the Faculty.

10. All persons elected to Fellowships are required, upon accepting their appointment, to file a bond to repay the University, in case of their resignation before the expiration of the time for which they were appointed, any sums which they may have received.

11. In all cases where Fellowships are not awarded, or when from any cause the income of one or more Fellowships may cease to be paid, or when the aggregate sum paid shall be less than the amount contemplated by this act, the surplus thus accruing shall be added to the principal of the loan fund for needy and meritorious students.

12. Either or both of the President White Fellowships in History and Political Science may in the discretion of the Faculty be made a travelling Fellowship for the purpose of study and investigation, the holder thereof making from time to time to the Faculty such reports of his progress as may be required. In case of a student of very exceptional ability and promise in the fields of either of these Fellowships, the two Fellowships may, in the discretion of the Faculty, for the sake of enabling very thorough research, be combined for a single year into one.

13. The three Susan Linn Sage Fellowships in Philosophy and Ethics shall be awarded by the General Faculty on the recommendation of the Faculty of the Susan Linn Sage School of Philosophy.

XVI.—SCHOLARSHIPS.

1. There have been established by the University thirty-six University Scholarships, and six Susan Linn Sage Scholarships, each of the annual value of $200.

2. The University Scholarships are named as follows: The Cornell Scholarships; the Lord Scholarships; the McGraw Scholarships; the Sage Scholarships; the Sibley Scholarships; the President White Scholarships; the Horace Greeley Scholarships; the John Stanton Gould Scholarships; and the Stewart L. Woodford Scholarships.

3. The University Scholarships are given:

(a) For the first two years of any course, on the basis of excellence in special examinations held at the beginning of the Freshman year.

(b) For the third and fourth years, on the basis of highest general standing in the first two years, including all the required work, and as much elective work as may be necessary to complete an aggregate amounting to sixteen hours a week taken in the University during two years. Work for which credit is given in consequence of having been done before coming to the University, is not to be considered in the computation.

4. Applicants for a University Scholarship must be free from conditions at the time of making application.

5. University Scholarships for the first two years will be given for passing examinations which shall average the highest in any three of the following groups, of which group (a) must be one:

(a). Arithmetic, and algebra through quadratic equations;

(b). Plane and solid geometry;

(c). Greek;

(d). Latin;

(e). French;

(f). German.

6. The holder of a University Scholarship shall forfeit the right to the same in case said holder shall at any time change the course in which he or she was registered at the time of receiving the award, unless the records of entrance examinations shall show that, at the time of the holder's admission to the University all the subjects required for admission to the course last chosen were passed by him or her; and all candidates must state before the Scholarships are awarded what course they intend to pursue.

7. The holders of University Scholarships must be candidates for the first degree, and shall not be recommended by the Faculty for such degree, except after a residence of the full period of four years at the University.

8. All persons shall be debarred from the competition for University Scholarships, for the first two years of any course, who shall have participated in any previous competition for the same, or shall have been in any previous year or years registered as a student in this University, or in any other University or College.

9. A University Scholarship will be forfeited at any time in case two-thirds of the Faculty present at any meeting, notice having been given at the meeting immediately before, shall decide that the holder has been guilty of negligence, or of conduct of any kind that is unbecoming a student holding such Scholarship.

10. Whenever any University Scholarship shall for any reason become vacant, the vacancy can be filled by the Faculty only from the students of the same course as that in which the vacancy occurred.

11. The Susan Linn Sage Scholarships are awarded by the General Faculty on the recommendation of the Faculty of the Susan Linn Sage School of Philosophy; and are awarded to students who have already taken the baccalaureate degree, and are pursuing studies in philosophy and ethics with a view to a higher degree.

12. The moneys due on Scholarships are paid at the office of the Treasurer of the University in three equal payments, on 15th of December, 15th of March, and 15th of June.

XVII.—MISCELLANEOUS PROVISIONS.

1. All graduates of the first degree, in any of the departments of Cornell University, and all persons who have been admitted to any degree higher than the first in the University shall be Alumni of said University, and as such shall be entitled to vote for Alumni Trustees under and in pursuance of the provisions contained in Chapter 763 of the Laws of New York passed in 1867, and the amendments thereof.

2. Any student of the University who, since receiving the degree of B.M.E. or B.C.E., has had three years or more of reputable study or practice in the profession of Mechanical or Civil Engineering, may, on the recommendation of the Director of his College, and on payment of the fee required for a first degree and all other dues, be admitted to the degree of Mechanical Engineer or Civil Engineer, and the President is authorized to sign the proper diploma.

3. In addition to the powers and duties in the foregoing provisions, the various persons, officers, faculties, and committees shall continue to exercise the powers and be subject to the duties heretofore enjoyed or imposed by usage, custom, and ordinary practice in so far as they may not conflict with the positive legislation herein contained; and

any other powers that shall be necessary and proper for carrying into effect these provisions. And the Executive Committee may make new rules or modify, when necessary, the foregoing regulations by a two-thirds vote.

4. All ordinances or resolutions prior to August 1, 1890, relating to the subjects contained in this revision are repealed, but such repeal shall not affect or apply to any resolution or ordinance of a personal, local, or temporary nature.

[No. 1.]

VOTES OF THE GENERAL FACULTY, CORNELL UNIVERSITY.

Nov. 30, 1888.

[Amended Dec. 7, 1888.]

The Faculty recommend to the Executive Committee of the Board of Trustees, that the following limitations be added to the conditions of scholarship competition already in force :

1. Persons over 21 years of age shall be debarred from the competition.

2. The holder of a scholarship shall forfeit the rights to the same, in case said holder shall at any time change the course in which he or she was registered at the time of receiving the award, unless the record of entrance examinations shall show that at the time of the holder's admission to the University, all the subjects required for admission to the course last chosen were passed by him or her. All candidates must state before the scholarships are awarded what course they intend to pursue.

3. Holders of scholarships must be candidates for a first degree, and shall not be recommended by the Faculty for such a degree, except after the full period of four years' residence at the University, and after having pursued in the University all the courses of study leading to the degree.

4. All persons shall be debarred from the competition for the University scholarships who shall have participated in any previous competition for the same, or who shall have been in any previous year or years registered as a student in this University, or any other university or college of similar standing.

5. These resolutions do not take effect until 1891.

[The above action was presented to the Executive Committee and by them confirmed Nov. 4, 1889.]

VOTES OF THE GENERAL FACULTY, CORNELL UNIVERSITY.

1. Any student registered as Senior in one of the four-year courses leading to a degree may be a competitor, provided he has taken at least one course of instruction in Elocution.

2. Every competitor shall be required to submit, at the Registrar's office, on or before noon of the first Monday of the Spring term, an original oration upon a subject which shall have previously been approved by the Professor of Rhetoric.

3. The competing orations shall be limited to fifteen hundred words ; shall be written with a type-writer ; shall be signed with a fictitious name ; and be accompanied with a sealed envelope containing the fictitious name of the writer without, and the real name within.

4. From the orations submitted, a Committee appointed by the Faculty shall select the best, not to exceed six in number, for delivery in public, and the names of the successful writers shall be announced as early as is practicable after the beginning of the Spring Term.

5. The prize shall not be conferred unless the successful competitor shall complete his course and take his degree at the Commencement next following.

6. The contest for the prize will take place on the evening of the Wednesday preceding Commencement Day, under the direction of the President of the University.

7. The prize shall be awarded by a Committee of three appointed by the President from persons not resident in Ithaca, whenever practicable.

8. A copy of each of the orations selected for the competition shall, within one week after the selection, be deposited by its author with the committee charged with the selection, who shall, after the com-

pletion of the competition, deposit the successful oration permanently in the University Library.

RULES AS TO COMMENCEMENT SPEAKERS, RE-AFFIRMED JAN. 10, 1890.

1. Any member of the Senior class who is to receive a degree on the coming Commencement may compete for a place on the Commencement stage, providing proof of satisfactory oratorical ability has been given to the teacher of Elocution and Oratory.

2. Each competitor must present at the Registrar's office, at or before noon of the last Friday in April, a production of no more than 750 words on any subject approved by the head of the department in which the subject lies.

3. From such productions a Committee from the Faculty will select no more than nine to be delivered on the Commencement stage.

RESOLUTIONS AS TO THE DEGREE OF BACHELOR OF SCIENCE IN ARCHITECTURE, PASSED FEB. 21, 1890.

Resolved, That the degree of Master of Science in Architecture be conferred upon candidates, who, having previously taken the degree of Bachelor of Science in Architecture in this University, spend one year in study at the University, and comply with the other requirements for the Master's degree.

Resolved, That the following changes be made in the Register. On page 154, line 6 of the first clause under the heading " Advanced Degrees," and also on page 155, line 5, after the word " Engineering," insert the word "Architecture." On page 88, line 10, insert the word "Architecture" before the word " and."

RESOLUTION AS TO STUDENTS TAKING WORK IN THE LAW SCHOOL, PASSED FEB. 21, 1890.

Resolved, That the resolution reported to the Faculty, Oct. 7, 1887, (Faculty Records, C. 251), and then adopted, be amended to read as follows : " Undergraduates in any other department of the University shall not be permitted to take studies in the Law School except by special permission of the General Faculty, to be obtained from term to term."

GENERAL LEGISLATION OF THE FACULTY AND EXTRACTS FROM THE FACULTY RECORDS.

MISCELLANEOUS SELECTIONS.

SEPT., 1868—OCT., 1890.

FACULTY PROCEDURE AND RULES.

Fac. B, page 208.   Feb. 18, 1876.

Voted, That hereafter the Faculty meet at 4 o'clock on Fridays and adjourn not later than 6 o'clock.

Voted, That in the discussions of the Faculty no member be allowed to speak more than twice on the same motion at any one meeting, without special permission of the Faculty.

Voted, That no rule of the Faculty shall be suspended except by a two thirds vote of the members present.   .

Fac. A, page 277.   April 26, 1872.

Voted, That when the Faculty adjourn, it be to meet on Thursday evening at 7½ o'clock, and that less than a quorum be deemed sufficient to transact the business of the meeting.

Fac. C, page 234.   June 13, 1887.

Resolved, That in the opinion of the Faculty it is desirable that the offices of Secretary and Registrar be combined.

Fac. B, page 128.   Sept. 11, 1874.

1. *Resolved*, That the following committees be established as standing committees of the Faculty, to wit:

(a) A committee on entrance examinations, consisting of the Registrar, the associate professor of history, and the professors of rhetoric and mathematics.

(b) A committee on term examinations, consisting of the Vice President, the Registrar, and five professors.

(c) A committee on registration, consisting of the Vice President and two professors.

(d) A committee on qualifications for graduation, consisting of the Vice President, Registrar, and five professors.

II.

(e) A committee on the exemption of laboring students from the full amount of University services required, consisting of three professors.

(f) The military committee, consisting of the professor of military science and two other professors.

(g) A committee on the publication of the Register, consisting of the Registrar, the Secretary of the Faculty, and the professor of rhetoric.

2. The members of these committees, in all cases except those that are described by their offices as members *ex officio*, shall be appointed annually by the presiding officer at the first regular meeting of the Faculty after the Summer vacation.

3. The President is *ex officio* a member of each of the above committees.

[For action establishing these and other committees of the Faculty, see Reprints of Faculty Legislation, p. 27.]

Fac. B, page 187.   Oct. 15, 1875.

Voted, That all applications and communications from students to the Faculty must be made in writing.

Fac. A, page 17.   Nov. 18, 1868.

Resolved, That no anonymous communications to the Faculty be received, but that the same be destroyed by the Secretary, and that notice of this resolution be given to the students.

Fac. A, page 157.   Nov. 11, 1870.

Voted, That hereafter all motions and amendments to motions that are not merely the granting or refusing of a written application shall be in writing, dated and signed by the person making the motion or amendment.

Fac. A, page 273.   April 12, 1872.

Voted, That hereafter when any resolution has been offered, any amendment that relates to the same subject matter shall be in order.

Fac. B, page 216.   April 14, 1876.

Resolved, That no motion or resolution affecting the general policy of the University shall be put on its passage till the same shall have been referred to a committee and reported upon at a specified subsequent meeting.

Fac. B, page 315.   Nov. 9, 1877.

Voted, That hereafter all subjects which are referred as the special order of the day at a certain future meeting be taken up, unless otherwise designated, immediately after reports on delinquent students.

III.

Fac. A, page 175.   Feb. 3, 1871.

Resolved, That the interests of the University require that the Faculty whenever it acts should act as a unit, and that the existence of differences of opinion among its members as to its action should not be known outside.

Resolved, That it is a breach of good faith in a member of the Faculty to allow the opinion of any other member on any matter which may have come before it to be known outside.

Fac. C, page 477.   March 7, 1890.

Moved and carried, That the discussions and doings of the Faculty as to discipline be considered wholly confidential.

REGISTRATION.

Fac. A, page 103.   Dec. 20, 1869.

Resolved, That each member of the Faculty be requested to demand from each student the certificate of registration at the beginning of each term, and to consider no student a member of his class without such certificate.

ABSENCES.

Fac. C, page 143.   Dec. 12, 1885.

The committee to whom was referred the resolutions in regard to attendance on University exercises reported, recommending the adoption of the following resolutions :

1. That, for the present, attendance at recitations and lectures be made voluntary for students of all classes ; provided that in case any student shall so neglect his work, by absence or otherwise, as to impair or endanger his own standing or the scholarship of his class, he may after due warning, with the approval of the head of the department in which the neglect occurs, and with the approval of the President of the University, be excluded from attendance in the class and from the ensuing examination.

That the President and Faculty desire it to be understood that this arrangement is regarded by them as an experiment, and that its success and final adoption as the method of the University will depend largely upon the intelligent and hearty co-operation of the students.

That the keeping of a record of absences be left to the discretion of heads of departments.

Fac. C, page 468.   Jan. 6, 1890.

Voted, That no doctor's certificate will be accepted by the Faculty without the endorsement of the professor of physical culture.

IV.

EXAMINATIONS.

Fac. A, page 11.   Oct. 21, 1868.

Voted, That all the students be examined at the end of the term on the studies of the term ; and that all who were conditioned on admission to the University be further examined at the same time in those studies in which they were conditioned. [Compare other resolutions on this subject.   Reprints, pp. 6, 21–26.]

Fac. A, page 181.   March 3, 1871.

1. *Resolved*, That the examinations be appointed to begin on the second Monday before the end of the term, and to continue daily until completed, and that they shall not extend beyond Saturday evening ; and that all recitations shall cease at the commencement of examinations.

2. *Resolved*, That each professor shall have the hours he has occupied during the term for examinations, or instead thereof at his option, three consecutive hours in the afternoon of any day, or in the forenoon of Saturday, to be arranged by a committee appointed for that purpose to avoid collisions.

Resolved, That every professor shall be liable to be assigned by the Faculty to attend any examination where his aid shall be needed by the professor of that department, provided the classes be examined in divisions of not less than 40 for the larger rooms and 21 in the long rooms.   [Modified later.   Compare Reprints, p. 26.]

Fac. C, page 41.   May 23, 1884.

The following resolutions in regard to reports of examinations were taken from the table and adopted :

1. That it is the duty of each member of the Faculty to deliver to the Registrar his report of an examination as soon as possible thereafter ; and that all absences from examinations shall be indicated in these reports.

2. That all examination reports must be handed to the Registrar within 3½ working days after the last day of examination.

3. That it shall be the duty of the Registrar to report at the next succeeding meeting of the Faculty the names of such members of the Faculty as have not complied with the foregoing resolutions.

4. That the Secretary of the Faculty is hereby instructed to mail a printed copy of these resolutions to each member of the Faculty.

Fac. C, page 188.   Oct. 22, 1886.

Resolved, That hereafter all reports of examinations made to the Registrar shall be in writing and on the official blanks provided therefor.

V.

Fac. A, page 282. May 17, 1872.

Voted, That when the report of any examination has been once made to the registrar, no change shall be made in it except by consent of the Faculty or some committee acting for the Faculty.

MISCELLANEOUS.

COEDUCATION.

Fac. A, page 266. March 22, 1872.

A communication was received from the Assistant Treasurer stating that the Executive Committee had passed the following resolution :

Resolved, That women be admitted to the University upon the same terms as men.

DRILL.

Fac. A, page 279. May 8, 1872.

The following resolutions reported from the Military Committee were passed :

Resolved, That students coming under the heads named below be excused from drill and military duty by the Military Committee, when application is made to them, and they on examination into the case are satisfied that the applicant for excuse belongs to either of the classes, namely :

1. Persons who are physically disabled ;
2. Persons who have conscientious scruples ;
3. Aliens, subject to foreign governments ;
4. Persons who have been in the U. S. service ;
5. Students in the labor corps, who need the time for their labor ;
6. Students who have had drill and military instruction elsewhere,— to the extent to which they have had such instruction ;
7. Students in the Senior class, who are not needed as officers, on condition of their studying and passing examination in tactics.

ATHLETICS.

Fac. C, page 227. May 20, 1887.

The following resolution was adopted :

Resolved, That while we are willing and anxious to do everything in our power to encourage the students of this University in their laudable efforts to distinguish themselves in all proper physical contests, nevertheless we regard it as essential to our success as an educational institution that the time consumed should not be too great, and that so far as possible such contests when not occurring in Ithaca should be held on the last day of the week.

VI.

Resolved, That the President and Dean be requested to grant leave of absence to attend physical contests or field sports only to such as are duly certified as contestants.

DISCIPLINE.

Fac. C, page 196. Jan. 7, 1887.

Resolved, That all cases of dropped students asking to be reinstated be referred back to the committee on doubtful cases with power.

Fac. A, page 160. Nov. 18, 1870.

Moved, That when a vote is passed by the Faculty whereby any punishment is inflicted upon a student, when said punishment makes it necessary for the student to leave the University, the Secretary of the Faculty shall send a notice of the same to the Business Manager of the University; and that it shall be the duty of the Corresponding Secretary to send a notice of the action of the Faculty to the parents or guardian of the student concerned, as soon as practicable, provided that no other provision be made for their notification in the measure itself. Passed.

Fac. B, page 326. March 1, 1878.

Voted, That whenever a student is suspended from the University or when any application of a student for readmission to the University is rejected, it shall be the duty of the Secretary to notify the parents or guardian of such student of the action of the Faculty.

Fac. A, page 155. Nov. 4, 1870.

Moved that in case of dismissal from the University, dismissal be of two classes : honorable dismissal and simple dismissal.

Fac. B, page 419. March 5, 1880.

A motion to the effect that smoking be prohibited in the halls and public rooms and around the doors of the University buildings was laid on the table.

Voted, That the Faculty suggest to its individual members to speak to students in regard to the impropriety of smoking in the halls and public rooms of the University.

SOCIETIES.

Fac. B, page 24, 1873.

The following resolutions were unanimously adopted :

(1) *Resolved,* That no secret society shall be allowed to remain or be established in the University, which shall not be shown to the satisfaction of the Faculty to be favorable to scholarship, good order, and morality, and to be free from all initiatory or other rites, cere-

monies, or proceedings, dangerous, degrading, or unworthy of gentlemen and members of an institution of learning.

(2) *Resolved*, That no student be allowed to become or to remain a member of any society publicly condemned by the Faculty ; and no person shall receive an honorable dismission or any degree who shall not at the time of applying for the same satisfy the Faculty that he has not violated this rule.

(3) *Resolved*, That no association of students for the mere purpose of initiation, nor mock societies, shall be allowed in this University, and that any student who shall join any such association or mock society, knowing it to be such, or engage in any of its initiation proceedings, or in any proceedings of the nature of mock initiations shall be suspended or expelled from the University.

(4) *Resolved*, That nothing contained in these resolutions shall be held to restrict the Faculty from further action regarding college societies, should the present action be found ineffectual.

SCHOLARSHIPS.
Fac. C, page 289.   Feb. 2, 1888.

The question having been raised, the chair ruled that a student suspended from the University did not forfeit his scholarship, in case he held one, unless definite action to that effect was taken by the Faculty.

CERTIFICATES.
Fac. C, page 244.   Sept. 30, 1887.

The following resolution was adopted :
Diplomas and certificates of all kinds must be presented at or before the time for examination for admission to the University, in order to be accepted in lieu of requirements either for entrance, or for work toward graduation.

TECHNICAL STUDIES.
Fac. C, page 59.   Oct. 3, 1884.

Resolved, That students not registered in technical courses may be admitted to studies in such courses only by consent of the professor in charge of the department affected, or by vote of the General Faculty. The head of the department shall have power to prescribe the order and method of studies of those who are thus admitted.

COURSE IN ARTS.
Fac. B, page 26.   Feb. 29, 1884.

The following resolution was adopted :
That the course in Arts is regarded by this Faculty as a distinctly classical course, and Greek as its characteristic study ; and in view of

the other degrees conferred by the University it is assumed that students offering themselves as candidates for the degree of Bachelor of Arts have thereby expressed a preference for classical studies and especially for the study of Greek.

DEGREES.

Fac. A, page 204. June 9, 1871.

The committee upon the gradation of degrees reported :

That they do not deem it expedient to make any distinction of the kind, as such grading would involve the evil of the prize system, viz., that of encouraging cramming rather than honest work for the love of it.

Fac B, page 174. June 11, 1875.

Resolved. That the Faculty do not recommend any diploma to be antedated.

ALUMNI.

Fac. C, page 315. May 11, 1888.

The committee appointed to prepare a recommendation to the Board of Trustees as to who should be considered Alumni of the University, presented the following report, which was accepted and adopted :

WHEREAS, The charter of this University confers upon the authorities of the institution the power of defining the meaning of the word "alumnus" so far as the term may authorize the right to vote for a Trustee of the University ; and

WHEREAS, The term alumnus has never been authoritatively defined ; and

WHEREAS, The establishment of new schools in the University is likely to raise the question as to the right of graduates of such schools to vote for the Trustees ; therefore

Resolved, That the Faculty recommend to the Board of Trustees the adoption of a rule conferring the right to vote for Trustees upon the following classes of persons :

1. All persons who have taken a degree at the University for which the regularly prescribed course of study is at least four years in length.

2. All persons who have taken a second degree in the University after having taken a baccalaureate degree requiring at least four years of study in another institution.

GENERAL LEGISLATION OF THE FACULTY AND EXTRACTS FROM THE FACULTY RECORDS.

OCT. 1ST, 1890—DEC. 12TH, 1890.

Admission on Certificate.—The Dean, Professors Wilder, Wait, Wheeler, Hart. [Records C, 165–166, 296, 309].

Graduate Work and Advanced Degrees.—Professor Hewett, the Dean, Professors Fuertes, Thurston, Wait, Hale, Tyler. Professor Tyler resigned from the Committee October 17th, and Professor Tuttle was chosen to fill the vacancy. [Records C, 181, 186, 198, 245, 251, 496].

Doubtful Cases.—The Dean, Professors Babcock, Fuertes, Crane, Thurston, Hale, Hitchcock, Jones, Gage. [Records A, 267 ; B, 32, 46].

Advanced Standing.—The Dean, Professors Caldwell, Fuertes, Thurston, Crane, Oliver, S. G. Williams, Schurman, Bristol. [Records C, 208–209].

Changes in Registration—Including Extra and Deficient Hours. —The Dean, the Secretary, and the heads of the departments concerned. [Records C, 195, 271, 443].

Register and Announcement of Courses.—The President, the Dean, the Registrar.

Scholarships.—Professors H. S. Williams, Wilder, Hewett, Jones, Bristol. [Records C, 225].

Records of Candidates for Graduation.—The Dean, Professors Caldwell, Fuertes, Tuttle, Wait, Thurston, Schurman, Wheeler. [Records C, 145, 174, 229, 267].

Military and Gymnasium Committee.—The Dean, the Commandant, and the Professor of Physical Culture, *ex-officio.* [Records C, 302, 321].

Athletics.—Professors Hitchcock, White, Wheeler, Kemp. [Records C, 437].

Records C, p. 514.

Iu the case of students desiriug teachers' certificates, or mention in diplomas of work done during the Junior and Senior years, the following clause is to be added to the rules on pages 65 and 121 of the Register for 1890–1891, viz. :

The applicant is to take an average of at least five hours of work throughout the two years, and in no term is to fall below four hours. The word " continuously," on page 121, is to be omitted.

THANKSGIVING RECESS.

Records C, p. 514.

The action of the Faculty of November 22, 1889, (Records C, p. 463), regarding the Thanksgiving Recess, is adopted as the permanent policy of the Faculty. The days thus set apart for the recess are to be designated in the University Calendar as printed in the Register.

REGULATIONS FOR THE MASTER'S DEGREE.

Records C, p. 515.

The rule for examinations for the Master's Degrees is so amended as to require such candidates to present one major and one minor subject.

CREDIT FOR WORK DONE IN THE SCHOOL OF LAW BY STUDENTS IN OTHER DEPARTMENTS OF THE UNIVERSITY, AND FOR WORK DONE IN OTHER DEPARTMENTS BY STUDENTS IN THE SCHOOL OF LAW.

Records C, pp. 519, 520.

As a result of the conference with the Faculty of the Law School, voted that the action of the Faculty taken Feb. 21, 1890, (Records C, p. 475), be amended as follows :

I. Undergraduates in any other department of the University shall not be permitted to receive credit for studies in the Law School except by recommendation of the General Faculty, and the permission of the Law Faculty, to be obtained from term to term.

II. Students in the Law School shall not be permitted to receive credit for studies in any other department of the University, except in the School of History and Political Science, without the recommendation of the Faculty of Law and the permission of the General Faculty, to be obtained from term to term.

Records C, p. 521, a.

Resolutions adopted by the Board of Trustees at their meeting, October 22d, 1890 :

Resolved, That upon the completion of the new Agricultural Building, the existing provision with reference to the admission of Agricultural students free from tuition, beyond the State Scholarships, be and is hereby rescinded.

Resolved, That whenever any full professorship is to be filled, the President of the University shall, upon request of the Board of Trustees, or of the Executive Committee, seek diligently and to the best of his ability, and bearing in mind the provision of the fundamental charter of this University, which forbids him to take cognizance of any political or religious views which any candidate may or may not hold, shall nominate to the Senate the person whom he shall consider most worthy to occupy the vacancy to be filled. Thereupon the Senate, after proper deliberation, shall vote by ballot yea or nay upon the recommendation, and their action, with any reasons for it which the Senate may see fit to submit, shall be certified to the Board of Trustees, who shall then confirm or reject such nomination.

Said confirmation or rejection to be by ballot, said ballot to be not by a single open vote to be cast by any one person, but by the ballots of all present and voting.

DEGREES OF "MASTER OF PHILOSOPHY," AND OF "MASTER OF LETTERS."

Records C., p. 525.

The Committee on Graduate Work and Advanced Degrees recommend the establishment of the degrees of Master of Philosophy, and Master of Letters, to be conferred upon Bachelors of Philosophy and of Letters, on terms similar to those which the degrees of Master of Arts, and Master of Science are now conferred. The report of the Committee was adopted.

REGULATIONS CONCERNING THESES.

Records C., p. 526. See also Records C., p. 488.

I. The Registrar shall submit to the Faculty before the balloting for degrees, a list of all theses which have been handed to him under the regulations of the Faculty, and the Registrar shall be made responsible for the deposit of said theses in the University Library.

II. A standard form and size for theses is adopted, said size to be eight by ten and one-half inches.

III. The diploma for the Doctor's degree shall be withheld until the required number of printed copies of the thesis is deposited in the University Library.

IV. After the theses have been received at the Library, they shall be permitted to circulate, subject to such regulations as may be in force concerning printed works.

V. In the regulations touching the graduation thesis, given on page 153 of the Register, it shall be stated that the copy of the thesis presented to the Faculty, shall, if accepted, become the property of the University.

EXEMPTION FROM DRILL OF STUDENTS WHO WORK FOR THEIR SUPPORT.

Records C., pp. 526, 529.

The phrase in rule 28 for the guidance of students—"students obliged to work for their support,"—shall be construed to imply that such students, in order to be entitled to exemption from drill, are to establish the fact that they are so engaged for not less than ten hours per week.

THE REGULATIONS FOR THE DEGREE OF DOCTOR OF SCIENCE.

Records C., p. 531.

The degree of Doctor of Science is conferred upon graduates of this University, and of other institutions whose course of study for the baccalaureate degree is substantially equivalent to the courses for the degree of Bachelor of Science in this University, and who are prepared to pursue advanced work in Chemistry, Physics, Mathematics, or Natural History, on the following conditions :

I. The candidate must possess a knowledge of Latin and Greek at least equivalent to that required for graduation with the degree of Bachelor of Science in Natural History.

II. He must spend at least two years at the University pursuing a course of study marked out by the Faculty in the departments of Chemistry, Physics, Mathematics, or Natural History.

III. He must present a thesis of such a character as shall display power of original and independent investigation, and must pass the requisite special final examinations.

RULES FOR CANDIDACY FOR ADVANCED DEGREES AND FOR GRADUATE STUDY.

Records C, p. 533.

Graduates in the several courses of this University, or of institutions offering courses substantially equivalent, will, upon the recommendation of the Committee on Graduate Work, be admitted to

graduate study, and may also, on recommendation of the same committee, be admitted to candidacy for an advanced degree in any department in which they are prepared to enter upon advanced work, subject, however, to the following condition : In case the requirements of the course in which the applicant has been graduated are essentially different from those demanded in this University for the first degree corresponding to that for which he applies, he will be obliged to make up such deficiencies before being admitted to his final examination.

COMMUNICATION FROM THE EXECUTIVE COMMITTEE.—THE UNIVERSITY SENATE.

Records C, p. 535, a.

I. The University Senate shall consist of the President of the University, and all the full Professors.

II. It shall be the duty of the Senate to counsel and advise in regard to all nominations for professorships ; to consider and make recommendations in regard to such courses of study as may pertain to more than one faculty of the University ; and, in general, to consider and make recommendations upon any question of University policy that may be submitted to this body by the Trustees, or the President, or either of the faculties.

III. The meetings of the Senate may be called by the President, or by the Secretary upon the written application of any five members ; and at such meetings the President, or in his absence the Dean of the General Faculty, shall preside. The Senate shall have a Secretary, whose duty it shall be to keep a record of proceedings, and to call all meetings under the direction of the proper authority.

GENERAL LEGISLATION OF THE FACULTY AND EXTRACTS FROM THE FACULTY RECORDS.

JAN. 9TH,—MARCH 13TH, 1891.

ALIENS AND MILITARY SCIENCE.

Records C, p. 539.

Aliens shall take Military Science or offer a substitute therefor.

REPORTS OF STANDING TO BE MADE EACH TERM.

Records C, p. 539.

Resolved, that in each subject the standing of every student shall be reported term by term, unless the Faculty authorize the deferring of such report.

[Compare cognate resolutions on this subject. Records C, p. 41.]

ASTHENIC CLASS IN PHYSICAL CULTURE.

Records C, p. 540.

The committee (appointed under a resolution of Professor Hitchcock, on Dec. 12, 1890, Records C, p. 537,) recommended that the rule (requiring work of Sophomores and Freshmen in the Gymnasium) be not changed, but that for the present term the classes be excused from exercise, and that the asthenic class be required to exercise five times a week through the term. Adopted.

AMENDMENT TO RULES FOR THE WOODFORD PRIZE COMPETITION.

Records C, p. 542.

The following substitute for Condition 1, on page 146 of the *Register*, was adopted : Any member of the Senior class who is to receive a degree at the coming Commencement may be a competitor, provided he has taken, at least, one course of instruction in Elocution and Oratory.

STUDENTS FAILING IN EXAMINATIONS.

Records C, pp. 542, 540.

Rule 15 for the guidance of students was amended to read as follows :

A student whose term examinations show that his average proficiency is not satisfactory, will be considered as being thereby

suspended from the University ; he will not be permitted to register again, except for special reasons, until the following year, at the beginning of the term corresponding to that in which the failure occurred, and in a subsequent class. If, after this, he again falls out of his classes, he will be readmitted only by special permission of the Faculty.

LEAVING TOWN FOR CLASS BANQUETS.

Records C, p. 543.

Action on a petition of the classes of '93 and '94. "While the Faculty appreciates the good spirit shown by the Sophomore and Freshman classes in their communication to the Faculty, yet in its opinion it is inexpedient to grant requests of classes to leave town for the purpose of holding class banquets."

THE COLUMBIAN EXPOSITION.

Records C, p. 543.

Resolved, that a committee of three professors in the general courses, and an equal number in the technical courses, be appointed by the chair for the purpose of making such provisional study and necessary recommendations as they may deem best for the appointment of a larger committee to take steps to represent this University in a proper manner at the Columbian Exposition, to be held at Chicago in 1893.

Records C, p. 548.

The committee on Columbian Exposition made a preliminary report, was enlarged to nine and continued. Voted that it is the sense of the Faculty that the University should be represented at the Columbian Exposition.

PUBLICATION OF A WEEKLY BULLETIN.

Records C, p, 546.

Resolved, that the President be requested by the Faculty to arrange for the issue of an official weekly bulletin, containing announcements for the week succeeding the date of issue.

RULES FOR STUDENTS IN THE COURSES IN HISTORY, LETTERS, SCIENCE, NATURAL HISTORY.

Records C, p. 548.

The rule requiring that nine hours of work be elected continuously during the last two years in the courses in History and Political Science, Letters, Science, and Natural History, (see *Register* of 1890–1891, pp. 122, 124, 125,) is construed to mean nine hours per term, with not less than seven hours in any one term.

GENERAL LEGISLATION OF THE FACULTY AND EXTRACTS FROM THE FACULTY RECORDS.

STANDING COMMITTEES OF THE FACULTY, 1891–92.

Admission on Certificate.—The Dean, Professors Wilder, Oliver, Wheeler, Hart.

Advanced Standing.—The Dean, the Registrar, Professors Caldwell, Fuertes, Thurston, Crane, Wait, S. G. Williams, Schurman, Jenks.

Graduate Work and Advanced Degrees.—Professor Hewett, the Dean, Professors Fuertes, Thurston, Wait, Hale, Tuttle, Laughlin.

Doubtful Cases.—The Dean, the Registrar, Professors Babcock, Fuertes, Crane, Thurston, Hitchcock, Newbury, Jones, Gage.

Changes in Registration—Including Extra and Deficient Hours. —The Dean, the Secretary, and the heads of the departments concerned.

Register and Announcement of Courses.—The President, the Dean, the Registrar.

Scholarships.—Professors H. S. Williams, Wilder, Crane, Hewett, Wait, Wheeler, Newbury.

Records of Candidates for Graduation.—The Dean, the Registrar, Professors Caldwell, Fuertes, Tuttle, Wait, Thurston, Schurman, Wheeler.

Military and Gymnasium Committee.—The Dean, the Commandant, and the Professor of Physical Culture, *ex officio.*

Athletics.—Professor Hitchcock, the Commandant *ex officio*, Professors White, Wheeler, Dennis.

Assignment of Freshmen.—Professor Jones.

Excusing Labor Students.—Professors Comstock, Gage, Burr. [Records D, 24.]

Discipline.—The President, Professors Babcock, Roberts, Wheeler, White. [Records D, 40, 43.]

RULES CONCERNING UNIVERSITY SCHOLARSHIPS.

Records D, p. 18.

Voted concerning rule 4 in the regulations for University Scholarships, that the word "conditions" used therein shall be considered to mean only such conditions as apply to the course of study in which the applicant is registered.

REGISTRATION DAYS.

Records D, p. 21.

Resolved, That hereafter at the beginning of the year two days may be taken for the registration of new students.

COMMITTEE ON ADMISSION BY CERTIFICATE.

Records D, p. 30.

Voted, that the Registrar be made *ex officio* secretary of the Committee on Admission by Certificate.

EXCUSES FOR LABORING STUDENTS.

Records D, p. 30.

Voted, that all petitions for excuse from drill, except those based on the ground that the petitioner is a laboring student, be referred to the Committee on Military Affairs; also, that the petitions of laboring students to be excused from work in the Gymnasium in the winter term be referred to the Committee on Excusing Laboring Students from Military Drill.

ENTRANCE EXAMINATIONS OUTSIDE ITHACA.

Records D, p. 32.

Resolved, That the Faculty deems it unadvisable, at present, to hold entrance examinations outside of Ithaca, inasmuch as the system of admission by certificate would seem to render such examinations unnecessary.

PASSING UP ENGLISH.

Records D, p. 36.

Resolved, That the privilege of passing up Freshman or Sophomore English be restricted to students admitted to advanced standing, to graduates of State Normal Schools, and to special students.

STANDING COMMITTEE ON DISCIPLINE.

Records D, p. 39.

There shall be a standing committee on discipline; the President to be *ex officio* a member and chairman, and to appoint the other

members. Charges against a student must be presented in writing to the President, whose duty it shall be to submit each case to the committee. The President shall have the power to summon the accused and the party presenting the charges to appear before the committee, with such witnesses as they may choose to bring. The President shall also notify the accused, that he may request any officer of instruction in the University to act as his adviser before the committee. If any member of the committee is selected, or any charges are presented by a member of the committee, the said member shall retire from the committee for the time being, and his place shall be filled by some member of the Faculty appointed by the President. The committee shall consider each case brought before it, take such evidence as can be had, decide by ballot its conclusion as to the guilt or innocence of the accused, and report to the Faculty with recommendations as to the penalty, if any, which, in its judgment, ought to be inflicted. In case the committee find the accused party to be guilty, the chairman shall notify him of the fact that he has the right of appeal to the Faculty.

DEATH OF PROFESSOR SHACKFORD.

Records D, p. 41.

Resolved, That the Faculty of Cornell University has heard with profound sorrow of the death of Charles Chauncy Shackford, a scholar, colleague, and gentleman, loved and respected by all who knew him. With his death this Faculty drops from its roll a name endeared to many of its present members during a long acquaintance, in which his ripe scholarship and his many virtues were fully appreciated by his numerous friends, colleagues, and pupils. His probity, ability, industry, affable character, and purity of life will be long remembered at this Institution, as one of the forces which helped to lay the foundations upon which this University has been built, and for the success of which he contributed a noble share with loyal devotion and untiring effort. This Faculty is pleased to see that the portrait of this distinguished man of letters presented by his students to the University realizes their expressed wishes, "that the presence of Professor Shackford in our Library among the worthies of Cornell should serve as an inspiration to the labors of succeeding generations of young men."

Resolved, That we tender to the widow and surviving family of Professor Shackford our sincere sympathy.

Resolved, That these resolutions be spread on the book of records of this Faculty, given to the press for publication, and a copy of them attested by the Secretary of the Faculty be delivered to the family of our departed colleague.

12

LATIN FOR ADMISSION TO COURSES IN LETTERS AND IN SCIENCE.

Records D, p. 43.

The following resolution was offered on January 15th, 1892 :

Resolved, That Latin be required for entrance to the courses in Letters and in Science.

The consideration of this resolution was made the special order for the next meeting.

DIPLOMAS FOR DOCTOR'S DEGREES.

Records D, p. 44.

Resolved, That the diplomas of the doctors' degrees include a clause designating the chief lines of work pursued in the candidacy for the degree.

LATIN FOR ADMISSION TO COURSES IN LETTERS AND IN SCIENCE.

Records D, p. 45.

The committee to whom was referred the resolution concerning changed requirements for admission to the courses in Letters and in Science, reported as a substitute therefor the following resolutions :

I. That for admission to the course in Science, an equivalent amount of Latin be made a fourth subject with German, French, and advanced mathematics. Two of these subjects shall be required for admission to the course, with the proviso that the full amount of modern languages and advanced mathematics required for graduation in the course be satisfied.

This resolution was adopted.

II. That in and after ——, the requirements for admission to the course in Letters be the same as those for admission to the course in Philosophy, omitting the requirements in Greek and Roman History.

This resolution was taken up and considered at length at the meeting of February 5th, 1892, and upon a vote then taken failed of adoption.

EXAMINATIONS FOR STATE SCHOLARSHIPS.

Records D, p. 47.

At the meeting of February 19th, 1892, the President made the following statement to the Faculty :

" I have addressed the following communication to the Superintendent of Public Instruction concerning the examinations for State Scholarships : ' After the examination in June, 1892, and until further notice, the examinations for State Scholarships in Cornell University will be in the following subjects : (1) English ; (2) Arithmetic ; (3) Algebra ; (4) Plane Geometry ; and (5) either Latin, French, or German, at the option of the student.'

13

By this requirement it will be seen that after the present year
geography, American history, and physiology are not to be required
at the State Scholarship examination. Examination in these subjects, however will be required at the University as heretofore, except in case of admission by certificate covering these subjects."

COMMENCEMENT REPRESENTATION OF SCHOOL OF LAW.

Records D, p. 52.

Resolved, That each year a committee from the Faculty of the
School of Law, of which committee the head of the department of
Elocution and Oratory shall be a member, select for Commencement
speakers no more than two seniors in the School of Law ; their orations not to exceed seven hundred and fifty words in length. Further, that in view of the admission of two speakers from the School
of Law to the Commencement stage, it be voted that the rules as to
Commencement speakers on page 171 of the Register be amended
by the substitution in rule three of the word "seven" for "nine."

COMMITTEE ON GRADUATE STUDENTS.

Records D, p. 53.

Resolved, That the admission and regulation of graduate students
be entrusted to a standing committee of seven members of which
the Dean shall be *ex officio* chairman.

SUMMER COURSES OF STUDY.

Records D, p. 52.

The following petition was read to the Faculty :

To the Executive Committee of the
Board of Trustees of Cornell University:

GENTLEMEN—The undersigned, professors and instructors in Cornell University, respectfully ask leave to use certain rooms and apparatus of the University during a part of the coming summer, for the
purpose of giving instruction in the following subjects :

     Mathematics,
     Chemistry,
     Philosophy,
     The English, French, and German languages,
     Botany,
     Physical Culture,
     Classical Archaeology.

Your petitioners ask to have these courses announced in the name
of the University, and to give them under the general direction of
the heads of the departments concerned, and subject to such regulations and restrictions as you may impose.

14

In particular they wish to be held personally responsible for the use and care of University property, to pay the cost of the announcements, and to bear all other expenses that may occur ; and they suggest, as a matter alike of security to the University and of convenience to themselves, that all tuition and laboratory fees be paid to the treasurer of the University.

Without excluding other pupils, these courses are offered for the special benefit of teachers in the schools from which this University draws its patronage ; and it is believed that, by reason of the more intimate relations so formed with the schools, and of the broader knowledge and better methods of instruction the teachers will acquire, the pupils of these schools will come here better prepared for their University work, and so a material advantage will result to the University.

It is a practical scheme of University Extension, by which the teachers themselves will be taught under University instructors, by University methods, with access to University libraries, museums, and laboratories, and that at the only time in the year when they are free from other pressing engagements. It follows the general plan so successful at Harvard.

The city of Ithaca is a pleasant place of residence, the cost of living in the summer is small, and your petitioners believe that, when this scheme of instruction is well established and has become widely known, a very considerable body of teachers will gather here every year ; and they are assured by heads of important departments that, when this body has once gathered, they will themselves be glad to join in the work of instruction.

> GEO. W. JONES, Assistant Professor of Mathematics,
> W. R. ORNDORFF, Assistant Professor of Chemistry,
> O. F. EMERSON, Assistant Professor of Rhet. and Eng. Phil.,
> J. E. CREIGHTON, Instructor in Sage School of Phil.,
> C. VON KLENZE, Instructor in German,
> W. W. ROWLEE, Instructor in Botany,
> E. HITCHCOCK, JR., Professor of Phys. Cult. and Hygiene,
> ALFRED EMERSON, Associate Professor of Class. Archaeology.

The Faculty then

Resolved, That the communication be submitted to the Executive Committee with the approval of the Faculty (with the exception of the clause running " your petitioners ask to have these courses announced in the name of the University, and to give them under the general direction of the heads of departments concerned"), provided that the plan be regarded, for the present, as an experiment and that the studies thus conducted be not treated as part of any regular University work.

GENERAL LEGISLATION OF THE FACULTY AND EXTRACTS FROM THE FACULTY RECORDS.

APRIL 8TH, 1892—MARCH 3D, 1893.

FRAUD CONCERNING WOODFORD ORATION, 1891.

Records D, p. 54.

The Special Committee of Investigation reported that had they been acquainted with the other oration on the same subject by a Mr. Nailer, at the time of selecting orations for the contest, they would have been sufficiently assured of the plagiarism on the part of Mr. Farber to throw out his oration. That, having carefully compared the two orations after the charge of plagiarism had been made in our college papers, they were all assured that said charge was well founded; the identity in the whole tenor of thought and in much of the expression, leaving no doubt in their minds as to plagiarism. That Mr. Farber's letters addressed to President Adams and to Professor Smith do not, in their opinion, serve to exculpate him nor even to extenuate his offence—he even admitting that he had memorized and spoken the other oration as a preparation for the writing of his own. That under these circumstances they recommend to the Faculty that Mr. Farber be asked to return the prize medal.

The report was adopted and the President authorized to make public the action of the Faculty.

EXTENSION OF TIME ON THESES.

Records D, p. 57.

It was voted that extension of time on Theses, involving laboratory or experimental work, may be granted by the heads of the departments concerned.

PASSING ENTRANCE REQUIREMENTS.

Records D, p. 59.

Students may be allowed to pass up subjects included among the entrance requirements, at the discretion of the heads of departments concerned.

16

MENTION OF THESES.

Records D, p. 59.

In the Commencement programme, special mention of thesis titles as heretofore made shall be omitted, but against the name of each member of the graduating class the title of the thesis shall be given.

CHANGE IN ENTRANCE LATIN.

Records D, p. 61.

The subjects of Sallust's Catiline and Vergil's Eclogues shall be no longer required for admission to the courses in Arts and Philosophy.

LATIN FOR ADMISSION TO THE COURSE IN LETTERS.

Records D, p. 63.

Voted that the action taken Jan. 22, 1892, with reference to Latin for admission to the course in Science (see page 12 above), be extended to the course in Letters.

Records D, p. 64.

The subject of Sallust's Catiline shall be no longer required for admission to the course in Architecture.

STUDENTS FAILING IN EXAMINATIONS.

Records D, p. 66.

Rule 15 for the guidance of students was amended to read as follows :

A student whose term examinations show that his average proficiency is not satisfactory, may be temporarily removed from attendance on his university duties; he will not be permitted to register again, except for special reasons, until the following year, at the beginning of the term corresponding to that in which the failure occurred, and in a subsequent class. If, after this, he again falls out of his classes, he will be readmitted only by special permission of the Faculty.

CREDIT FOR WORK.

Records D, p. 66.

Voted that in case a study running through more than one term be discontinued by any student, without permission or valid excuse, the Faculty may, at the request of the department affected, cancel the credit already entered for such partial work.

OFFICIAL EXAMINATION BOOKS.

Records D, pp. 62, 63, 67.

Voted that, for all written final and term examinations, an examination blank book shall be used, the form of which shall be determined

by the President of the University; also that the following petition, accompanied by a copy of the report of the committee appointed on this subject, be presented by the Faculty to the Executive Committee:

" WHEREAS, The Faculty of the University are convinced that the use of an official examination book, to be furnished and distributed by the University, is necessary in order to provide a proper safeguard against fraud in examination. The Faculty, therefore, petition your Honorable body to provide a supply of such examination books sufficient for all written final examinations."

RESOLUTION OF THE EXECUTIVE COMMITTEE.

Students in the University are required hereafter to purchase their examination books, the form of book, together with the rules and regulations governing its use, to be determined by the President and the Treasurer.

GRECIAN AND ROMAN HISTORY.

Records D, p. 69.

Voted that the course as now given be no longer required of Freshmen in Arts and Philosophy, and that the two hours thus left free be given up to the reading of Greek and Roman historians.

RESOLUTIONS ADOPTED ON THE RETIREMENT OF PRESIDENT ADAMS.

Records D, p. 69.

WHEREAS, President Charles Kendall Adams has severed his connection with this University, we, the Faculty, desire to express our sincere regret that he has found such action necessary, and our appreciation of the zeal and efficiency of the administration of his office.

Since his accession the growth of the University has been marvelous; large sums of money have been expended in increasing material facilities; departments already in existence have been enlarged, and new ones have been created; a flourishing School of Law has been developed; the requirements for admission to the University have been raised; a more liberal policy with respect to elective work has been inaugurated; the courses of instruction have been expanded and brought into a more orderly arrangement; the standard of scholarship has been greatly advanced, and graduate work has been effectively promoted in all departments; a closer connection between the University and the public school system of the State has been brought about; unfriendly movements in the Legislature have been warded off, and friendly advances from other quarters have been happily met and reciprocated.

In all these activities the President of the University must of necessity take a leading part; and we recognize his careful and successful guidance through it all.

-

18

We bespeak for him a like measure of success in future fields of usefulness to which he may be called, and assure him of our high regard and hearty good wishes that will follow him wherever he may go.

Signed by the Committee:

G. C. CALDWELL,
A. N. PRENTISS,
J. E. OLIVER,
T. F. CRANE,
R. H. THURSTON.

DEAN OF THE GENERAL FACULTY.

Records D, p. 71.

The President nominated Professor Horatio S. White as Dean of the General Faculty, and the nomination was confirmed.

SPECIAL SHORT COURSE IN AGRICULTURE.

Records D, p. 71.

Voted that in the event of the establishment of a short course in Agriculture, students pursuing said course be admitted during the coming year at sixteen years of age.

HONORABLE DISMISSAL AND LEAVE OF ABSENCE EXTENDING OVER TERM EXAMINATIONS.

Records D, p. 71.

All such petitions shall be referred to the President and the Secretary as a Standing Committee.

PETITIONS TO GRADUATES IN LESS THAN FOUR YEARS.

Records D, p. 71.

These shall be referred to the Dean and the Registrar, with power.

STANDING COMMITTEES OF THE FACULTY—1892–93,

Admission on Certificate—The Dean, Professors Wilder, Oliver, Bennett, Hart.

Advanced Standing — The Dean, the Registrar, Professors Caldwell, Church, Thurston, Crane, Wait, S. G. Williams, Prentiss.

Graduate Work and Advanced Degrees—The Dean, Professors Nichols, Thurston, Wait, Wheeler, M. C. Tyler, Comstock.

Doubtful Cases—The Dean, the Registrar, Professors Babcock, Church, Crane, Thurston, Hitchcock, Jones, Gage.

Records of Candidates for Graduation—The Dean, the Registrar, Professors Caldwell, Church, Tuttle, Wait, Thurston, Hart, Bennett.

19

Register and Announcement of Courses—The President, the Dean, the Registrar.

Change in Registration, including Extra and Deficient Hours—The Dean, the Secretary, and the heads of the departments concerned.

Scholarships—Professors Crane, Wilder, Hewett, Wait, Wheeler, Crandall, Ryan.

Military and Gymnasium—The Dean, the Commandant, the Professor of Physical Culture (*ex-officio*).

Athletics—Dr. Hitchcock, the Commandant (*ex-officio*), Professors White, Wheeler, Dennis.

Assignment of Freshmen—Professor Jones.

Excusing Labor Students from Drill and Gymnasium—Professors Comstock, Gage, Burr.

Discipline—Professors Babcock, Roberts, Wheeler, Hewett, S. G. Williams.

Honorable Dismissal and Leave of Absence—The President, the Registrar.

ADDITIONAL MATHEMATICAL REQUIREMENTS FOR ENTRANCE TO THE COURSES IN MECHANICAL AND ELECTRICAL ENGINEERING AND ARCHITECTURE.

Records D, pp. 78, 83, 85.

Voted that in and after June, 1894, the subjects of Higher Algebra and Plane and Spherical Trigonometry will be required for admission to these courses.

ACTION OF THE FACULTY CONCERNING THE ESTABLISHMENT AND MANAGEMENT OF A SUMMER SCHOOL OF STUDY.

Records D, pp. 79, 81, 84, 86.

Report of the Committee to whom was referred the matter of a Summer School, as adopted by the Faculty :

It is the belief of the Committee that the Summer School affords an opportunity to do marked service to the teachers of this and other States ; and that the University should not neglect this means of cultivating closer relations with the preparatory schools.

It is the opinion of the Committee that the work undertaken in the Summer School should be distinctively college or university work, and not such as is done by preparatory schools ; and that the courses offered should therefore correspond in grade to those of our regular curriculum.

Since certain subjects of the Freshman year are also included in our entrance requirements, and since it should be the object of the Sum-

mer School to offer these subjects to teachers and to advanced students, and not to those studying for admission to the university, be it

Resolved, That in case of subjects included in the entrance requirements for the University, a previous knowledge of the subjects should be exacted, such knowledge to cover substantially the same ground as the entrance requirement. But this resolution is not intended to exclude from these studies persons actually engaged in teaching, nor advanced students.

Resolved, That study pursued in the Summer School be not credited in hours required for graduation to candidates for the first degrees.

Resolved, That in case it seem expedient to establish a Summer School, in the opinion of the Faculty, no member of the body of instruction should be required to be responsible for the instruction in said school.

RESOLUTIONS PASSED BY THE BOARD OF TRUSTEES NOVEMBER 22, 1892, AND TRANSMITTED TO THE FACULTY DECEMBER 2, 1892.

1. That a Summer School be established by the University.

2. That, subject to such provision as the Executive Committee may deem necessary, the management of the Summer School, both on its financial and educational sides, shall be in the hands of the teachers who, however, are instructed to arrange their curriculum in harmony with the policy formulated by the Faculty in its resolutions of October 21, which have already been communicated to the Executive Committee.

FORM FOR THESES FOR DOCTORS' DEGREES.

Records D, p. 85.

Voted that on the title page of each thesis deposited in the University Library, shall appear the statement that the thesis was presented to the Faculty of Cornell University for the degree in question.

CONDITIONS FOR THE DEGREE OF DOCTOR OF SCIENCE.

Records D, p. 88.

Voted that the requirement of Latin and Greek, as indicated on page 48 of Register, 1892–93, be no longer required for this degree, and this shall effect degrees conferred after June, 1893.

PHYSICAL TRAINING IN FRESHMAN YEAR.

Records D, p. 87.

Voted that Physical Training be required four hours per week during the winter term of Freshman year; in those courses where it is now required two hours per week for the Freshman and two hours for the Sophomore year during the same term. One class shall be ex-

GENERAL LEGISLATION OF THE FACULTY AND EXTRACTS FROM THE FACULTY RECORDS.

MARCH 10, 1893—MAY 30, 1893.

RULES GOVERNING THE MANAGEMENT OF EXAMINATIONS.

Records D, pp. 95, 101, 102.

In response to a communication from certain students desiring to form an association for improving the ethical standards of the University,

Voted : that they be informed that the Faculty has learned of such action with gratification, and that any such movement will have its sympathy and coöperation.

After an exchange of various communications between students and Faculty, the following resolutions, the substance of which was suggested at mass meetings of students, were adopted :

(1) Each student must, in order to make his examination valid, affix the following form, with his signature thereto : "I have neither given nor received aid in this examination."

(2) The functions of the present committee on discipline of the Faculty, so far as jurisdiction in cases of fraud in examination is concerned, are suspended. The said functions are to devolve for one year upon a committee composed of the President of the University, and of four seniors, three juniors, two sophomores, and one freshman. The President of the University is to be chairman of the committee.

(3) The election of the student members of the said committee shall be held at a special election of each class early in the Fall term, except the freshmen, who shall not elect till the end of the term. Decisions of this committee shall be communicated by its presiding officer to the Faculty for final action.

(4) The Faculty will dispense with the presence of proctors at examinations to prevent dishonesty.

(5) This scheme shall take effect at the examinations of the present term.

EXTENSION OF TIME FOR THESES.

Records D, p. 97.

All petitions for extension of time for thesis work are to be referred to the heads of departments concerned, with power.

CREDENTIALS OF APPLICANTS FOR ADMISSION.

Records D, p. 98.

In response to a communication from certain school principals to the Faculty,

Voted: that every applicant for admission to the University be directed to secure a statement from the principal of the school in which he prepared, regarding the character and completeness of his preparation. The failure to produce such a statement, however, is not to operate as a bar to the admission of the applicant; but such omission is to be noted on his record.

ENTRANCE REQUIREMENTS IN ENGLISH.

Records D, p. 99.

(1) In Regents' diplomas presented during the years 1894-5, six academic English counts shall be required, including English composition, in order to satisfy the requirement for entrance English.

(2) In 1896, either six academic English counts, including English composition, or three full years of the English course established by the Regents, February 9, 1893, shall be required.

(3) In and after June, 1897, four full years of the English course established by the Regents February 9, 1893, shall be required in order to satisfy the entrance requirement in English.

(4) Candidates presenting Regents' diplomas from schools that have only a three years' course in English shall not be exempt from the entrance examination in that subject after September, 1896, unless they offer eight academic English counts.

[See page 21 above. It was decided at a later meeting that sections (3) and (4) should for the present not be promulgated.]

TITLES OF COMMENCEMENT THESES.

Records D, p. 101.

The titles of all theses presented for degrees shall be printed on the Commencement programme.

PETITIONS FROM ATHLETIC ORGANIZATIONS.

Records D, p. 101.

Petitions from the various athletic organizations shall hereafter be referred to the committee on athletics, with power.

CODIFICATION OF FACULTY RECORDS.

Records D, p. 105.

Voted: that the Dean be authorized to codify the Faculty records, and report at a later date.

GENERAL LEGISLATION OF THE FACULTY AND EXTRACTS FROM THE FACULTY RECORDS.

CREDIT FOR LATIN PERFORMANCES.

Records D, p. 106.

The matter of allowing credit for the work done in the preparation of a Latin play was referred to Professor Bennett, with power.

EXAMINATIONS FOR ADVANCED DEGREES.

Records D, p. 112.

Resolved, A. That in the final examination for advanced degrees the examination of theses shall regularly precede the further examination of the candidate.

B. That in case of students who take examination in a year subsequent to that in which the required amount of study has been completed, the special committee be authorized to arrange such examinations at any time during the University year; provided that two weeks notice shall be given to the chairman of the Committee on Graduate Work and Advanced Degrees.

COMMITTEE ON GRADUATE WORK.

Records D, p. 113.

Voted that the Committee on Graduate Work be increased in number of members from 7 to 9.

ENTRANCE EXAMINATIONS.

Records D, p. 116.

No member of the University, or applicant for admission, will be allowed to take any entrance examination without a formal permit. This permit must be obtained from the Registrar's office.

Each examiner shall be empowered to ask, through the Registrar, for the aid of three assistants, to be chosen by the Registrar from the younger members of the instructing force in such wise as to insure so far as possible the recognition of any undergraduates of the University who may be present at the entrance examinations.

25

ENTRANCE LATIN IN ARCHITECTURE.

Records D, p. 118.

On motion voted that Latin be no longer allowed as an alternative for French or German for admission to the course in Architecture.

DRILL.

Records D, p. 118.

It was voted that students who intend to retire from the jurisdiction of the General Faculty, after two years of study, shall not for that reason be excused from drill in their second year.

DEGREES FOR MEMBERS OF FACULTY.

Records D, p. 120.

In accordance with the recommendation of the Committee on Graduate Work it was voted "That it is not in accordance with the policy of this Faculty to grant degrees to members of their own body."

SUMMER SCHOOL.

Records D, pp. 120 121.

The Faculty votes to concur with the Faculty of the Summer School in recommending to the Board of Trustees that the direction of instruction in the Summer School be vested in the General Faculty.

The resolutions were then adopted as follows :

A. Regularly matriculated students of the University are allowed credit for work done in the Summer School in accordance with the following restrictions : Work in the Summer School may be allowed the same credit as the same amount and kind of work in the University ; but no student shall be allowed credit for more than eight University hours in any summer session.

B. Credit shall be given only for courses that have received the approval of the General Faculty.

C. The proposed credit shall be based upon the regular University examinations held at the beginning of the Fall Term. In subjects in which no regular examinations are held at that time, special examinations may then be given by the departments concerned.

2. Students of the Summer School not matriculated in the University may receive certificates of attendance and satisfactory work, duly signed by their instructors and by the president of the University.

26

EXAMINATIONS.

Records D, p. 121.

The recommendation of the student committee on discipline that hereafter students in written preliminary examinations be required to make the same declaration as in final examinations was adopted ; and also that violations shall be considered as coming under the jurisdiction of said committee.

ADVERTISEMENTS IN THE REGISTER.

Records D, p. 123.

Resolved, That the preparatory schools of Ithaca be permitted to insert in the Register, as heretofore, a joint slip descriptive of their facilities.   Resolution lost.

CALENDAR.

Records D, p. 124.

Resolved, That the Thanksgiving recess be limited to one day :
That the Fall term end as near the 23rd of December, and that the Winter term begin as near the 3rd of January as possible.
That instruction in the Spring term end on the Thursday preceding Commencement Day.
That Commencement Day be held on the Thursday nearest the 20th of June ; and that the entrance examinations in the fall begin on the Wednesday nearest the 18th of September, and instruction begin on Thursday of the following week.
That the present reservation of an examination week at the end of each term be discontinued.
That these resolutions go into effect with the beginning of the next calendar year, January 1, 1894.

THANKSGIVING.

Records D, p. 124.

Resolved, That in the opinion of the Faculty it would be inadvisable to grant leave of absence to students for the purpose of extending the Thanksgiving recess.

GENERAL LEGISLATION OF THE FACULTY AND EXTRACTS FROM THE FACULTY RECORDS.

JAN. 5TH, 1894—JUNE 15TH, 1894.

STANDING COMMITTEES OF THE FACULTY, 1893-4.

[The reference to the Faculty records indicate the origin and functions of the Committees.]

Admission on Certificate.—The Dean, Professors Wilder, Oliver, Hart, Bennett. [Records C, 165-166, 296, 309, D, 30.]

Advanced Standing.—The Dean, the Registrar, Professors Prentiss, Crane, Fuertes, Williams, Thurston, Wait, Creighton. [Records C, 208-209.]

Graduate Work and Advanced Degrees.—The Dean, Professors Caldwell, Fuertes, Comstock, Thurston, Wheeler, Nichols, Jenks, Wait. [Records C, 181, 186, 198, 245, 251, 496, D, 53, 113.]

Doubtful Cases.—The Dean, the Registrar, Professors Crane, Fuertes, Thurston, Hitchcock, Gage, Osborne, Jones. [Records A, 267, B, 32, 46.]

Records of Candidates for Graduation.—The Dean, the Registrar, Professors Caldwell, Oliver, Fuertes, Thurston, Hart, Burr, Bennett. [Records C, 145, 174, 229, 267.]

Register and Announcement of Courses.—The President, the Dean, the Registrar. [Statutes III, 6. Records C, 116, 247, 350, 445.]

Changes in Registration, including Extra and Deficient Hours.— The Dean, the Secretary, and the Heads of Departments concerned. [Records C, 195, 271, 443, D, 71.]

Scholarships.—Professors Crane, Wilder, Hewett, Wheeler, Wait, Crandall, Ryan. [Records C, 225.]

Military and Gymnasium.—The Dean, the Professor of Physical Culture, the Commandant. [C, 302, 321,]

Athletics.—Dr. Hitchcock, The Commandant, Professors White, Wheeler, Dennis. [Records C, 437.]

Assignment of Freshmen.—Professors Jones, Willcox. [Records C. ? D. 13, 74.]

27

28

Excusing Labor Students from Drill and Gymnasium.—Professors Comstock, Gage, Burr. [Records D, 24.]

Discipline.—Professors Wheeler, Hewett, Oliver, Roberts, Williams, [Records D, 40, 43.]

Leave of Absence.—The President, the Registrar. [Records D, 71.]

Summer School.—Professors Bennett, Caldwell, Burr, Bailey, O. F. Emerson. [Records D, 129.]

DOUBTFUL CASES.

Records D, p. 125.

All appeals from the action of the Committee on Doubtful Cases were recommitted to the same.

CODIFICATION OF FACULTY RECORDS.

Records D, p. 126.

The Dean presented the report on codification of the Faculty legislation as appears below. The report was accepted and the thanks of the Faculty were voted the Dean for his laborious and efficient work.

REPORT OF THE DEAN ON CODIFICATION.

In October, 1890, the Dean was requested to supervise the selection of extracts from the minutes of the Faculty to be printed from term to term. At the close of the last academic year he was authorized, at his own suggestion, to codify the Faculty Records from the beginning, a task upon which he had already been for some time engaged, and to report at a later date. He has accordingly examined the records from the opening of the University in Sept., 1868, until Oct., 1890; at the end of which period began the printing of selections from the minutes as above indicated. All votes, resolutions, or other memoranda during this long period, which seemed of value in tracing the development of the educational policy of the Faculty, or as indicating a drift or change of sentiment in that body with reference to the various subjects of interest arising during its deliberations, were marked. Action on various student petitions was occasionally noted when such action might seem instructive. Entries on such action have however in recent years become somewhat meager, as such petitions are now generally examined by committees and the action endorsed upon the petitions, which are filed alphabetically and chronologically.

All such marked passages were then drawn off in typewritten form upon separate sheets—over 1800 in number—with reference to the volume, page, and date of entry. To these were added captions—sev-

eral often being needed for a single sheet—and an alphabetical index was made for the whole series.

These sheets, which are enclosed in a number of pamphlet cases, contain with the accompanying index a fairly complete résumé of the more important proceedings of the Faculty. From this résumé a further selection has been made and printed for the use of the Faculty, embodying chiefly legislation of the procedure of the Faculty, together with a series of miscellaneous resolutions not elsewhere incorporated. It did not seem advisable to increase further the volume of this reprint, as much of the legislation has become obsolete or unnecessary or superseded, or appears in the official records of the University. Finally, to make the Faculty Minutes entirely complete and intelligible, reference must frequently be made to the special Faculty indexes, and to the Registers and other current publications of the University, which are cited in the proceedings from year to year.

DEAN'S OFFICE.

Records D, p. 128.

Moved and carried, that Professor W. F. Willcox, as Acting Dean, be added to the Committees on Advanced Standing and on Graduate Work, and have charge of the business of those committees.

2. That he have charge also of the matter of leaves of absence and late registration, so far as it is at present in the hands of the Dean.

3. That in the absence of the Dean the next person on the list of committees of which the Dean is chairman, shall officiate as temporary chairman.

ADDRESSES FOR REGISTERS.

(For outside inquirers).

Records D, p. 129.

Voted that, the Faculty gives its consent that the addresses of correspondents requesting Registers be furnished, if not inconsistent with the convenience of the Registrar's office.

GRADUATE WORK.

Records D, p. 131.

Resolved, That the time spent in study for the master's degree, whether that degree be taken or not, may be counted in the time required for the doctor's degree, provided the special committee in charge of the case approves, certifying the work done as suitable to such doctor's degree.

30

CONCERNING STUDENT OFFENDERS.

Records D, p. 132.

Resolved, That the Faculty assure the civil authorities of Ithaca of their desire to co-operate with them in procuring the detection and securing the conviction of the perpetrators of the crime committed in connection with the Freshman Banquet on Tuesday last.

Further resolved, That the Faculty once more formally declare that, while students who have been convicted of offences against law and order will also be subjected to the discipline of the University, it is not the business of the Faculty but of the civil authorities to preserve the peace and maintain the law, which, in the opinion of the Faculty, should be upheld against student offenders with the same impartial rigor as is shown towards other offenders.

REQUIREMENTS FOR ADMISSION AND DEGREES.

Records D, p. 137.

Action taken by the Faculty March 19, 1894, and based upon the report of the Committee of 9 appointed October 27, 1893.

1. The course in Letters shall be abolished, beginning with the class entering in 1896.

2. For the degree of Bachelor of Science a majority of the elective work shall be in natural science or mathematics, beginning with the class graduating in 1896.

3. The courses in Agriculture and Architecture shall remain as at present, with the degrees of Bachelor of Science in Agriculture and Bachelor of Science in Architecture.

4. (a) For the class entering in 1896 the entrance requirements in modern languages for the course in Science shall be increased so as to include two years of French or two years of German (viz., an amount equivalent to courses 1 and 2 in the University) instead of one year as at present.

(b) In and after 1897 the entrance requirements for the course in Science shall include two years of French and two years of German (viz., an amount equivalent to courses 1 and 2 in the University) and also the one year of additional mathematics (viz., solid geometry, advanced algebra, plane trigonometry).

(c) In place of a modern language requirement an equivalent amount of an ancient classical language may be offered for admission; provided that the full amount of modern languages required for entrance and for graduation be taken in the courses.

5. In and after 1896 the entrance requirement in French or German for the course in Philosophy shall be the same as that for the course in

31

Science (4 (a)) and the alternative in additional mathematics (viz., solid geometry, advanced algebra, plane trigonometry) shall be withdrawn.

6. In the courses in Arts and Philosophy the major part of the elective work shall be in literary, historical, philosophical, and mathematical subjects; but this resolution shall not affect the existing regulations in regard to electing studies in the School of Law.

AMENDMENT TO THE RULES FOR THE DEGREE OF D. SC.

Records D, p. 143.

In exceptional cases the year of graduate work in a University elsewhere may be accepted by a special vote of the Faculty in place of a year in this University.

THE STUDENT COMMITTEE ON *DISCIPLINE.

Records D, p. 146.

Resolved, That the faculty hereby express to the student committee on discipline their gratification as to the results of the committee's examination of all cases of fraud in examination brought before it, and their belief that by its action it has contributed to raise the standard of honor here in regard to University work.

Resolved further, That the Faculty hereby express their willingness to continue to vest the same functions as heretofore in the student committee beyond the original term of one year.

Resolved further, That the Faculty hereby express their willingness to vest in the student committee the initiation and consideration of all cases of University discipline under the same provisions.

The recommendation of the student committee on discipline that hereafter the students in all written recitations be required to make the same declaration as in final examinations was adopted. And also voted that all violations shall be considered as coming under the jurisdiction of said committee.

SPECIAL DISTINCTIONS.

Records D, p. 147.

Voted that all special distinctions attached to advanced degrees be abolished.

GRADUATE THESES.

Records D, p. 150.

Voted in accordance with the report of the committee on graduate work that a text-book presumably written and published without reference to the degree for which it is presented be not accepted.

32

THE PRESIDENT WHITE FELLOWSHIP.

Records D, p. 150.

Voted that the word *modern* in the title of the President White Fellowship in Modern European History be construed to include mediæval.

REVISION OF RULES FOR STUDENTS.

Records D, p. 151.

Voted that the matter of the revision of the rules for the guidance of students be referred back to the committee in charge with power to consider and incorporate such amendments as they deem expedient and then to issue the amended rules for provisional use at the beginning of the University year.

UNDERGRADUATE THESES.

Records D, p. 152.

Voted that the theses of undergraduates in the general courses be hereafter submitted on or before the 15th of October next preceding their graduation and that the thesis receive credit toward graduation as two hours of academic work each term of their senior year.

GENERAL LEGISLATION OF THE FACULTY AND EXTRACTS FROM THE FACULTY RECORDS.

JUNE 19, 1894—MARCH 8, 1895.

THE STUDENT COMMITTEE ON DISCIPLINE.

Records D, p. 152.

The following resolution from the Student Committee on Discipline was communicated :

The Student Committee on Discipline desires to thank the General Faculty of the University for their encouraging approval of its work during the present academic year, and to express its appreciation of the Faculty's sympathetic attitude toward it which has at all times promoted harmony between the two bodies. The Committee further-more desires to thank the Faculty for the confidence they have reposed in it by offering to extend its existence indefinitely, and to vest in it the initiative and consideration of all cases of University discipline.

With a due sense of the responsibility which it thus assumes, but feeling that such action has already been approved by the student body in mass meeting assembled, and that it will promote the develop-ment of student self-government in Cornell University, the Committee expresses its willingness to accept the enlargement of its functions thus offered it.

THE '94 MEMORIAL PRIZE.

Records D, p. 157.

The following conditions were submitted :

1. Any undergraduate student of Cornell University may become a competitor for this prize.

2. From the whole body of competitors there shall be selected by the Faculty of the University, in such manner as it may deem best, the debaters, not to exceed eight in number who shall take part in the final competition.

3. The final competition shall take place at a public debate to be held annually, under the direction of the President of the University, at such date and place and in such manner as shall be from time to time determined by the Faculty of the University.

34

4. The question for each competition shall be selected by the Professor of Oratory, subject to the approval of the Faculty of the University, and shall be publicly announced by him at least four weeks before the date set for each debate.

5. The prize shall be awarded by a committee of three judges appointed annually by the President of the University to that competitor who shall be deemed by them the most effective debater, account being taken both of his thought and of its expression.

Voted that this be made the action of the Faculty.

LAW SCHOOL PETITIONS.

Records D, p. 158.

Moved and carried, that all petitions from students in the Law School desiring to take work in the other courses be referred to the Law Conference Committee with power.

SUBSTITUTIONS FOR REQUIRED WORK.

Records D, p. 159.

Moved and carried, that all petitions involving substitution of work for required courses be referred to the Committee on Registration with power.

ATHLETICS.

Records D, p. 159.

The Committee on Athletics submitted the following resolution :

We do not regard any person as qualified to be a member of a University team who comes to the University without the intention of remaining at least one year, or who receives any remuneration or consideration of any sort for his services.

Voted that this be made the action of the Faculty.

DEATH OF OREN GIBSON HEILMAN.

Records D, p. 159.

The following resolution was adopted :

Whereas, God in His infinite wisdom hath deemed it wise to remove from our midst Oren Gibson Heilman, and

Whereas, We deeply feel the loss of one thus taken from the very threshold of a brilliant career, be it

Resolved, That we, the members of the Faculty of Cornell University, recognizing the manly character and christian spirit which he ever displayed, express to his family the recognition of our loss and extend to them our heartfelt sympathy.

35

FELLOWSHIPS AND SCHOLARSHIPS.

Records D, p. 160.

Voted that the Secretary be empowered to insert the detailed action of the Committee on Scholarships in the minutes of the meetings of May 4 and 11, 1894. [Records D, pp. 144-146.]

The Faculty at the meeting on May 4th adopted the following resolutions concerning the new fellowships and graduate scholarships recently established by the Board of Trustees, and directed the Secretary to transmit a copy of the action to the Executive Committee of the University as follows:

"The Faculty recommend that the thirteen fellowships and ten graduate scholarships be assigned as follows: (a) The thirteen fellowships to twelve groups of departments as hereinafter specified, viz.:

(1) Mathematics, ... 1
(2) Chemistry, ... 1
(3) Physics, ... 1
(4) Civil Engineering, ... 1
(5) Mechanical and Electrical Engineering, ... 2
(6) Physiology and Vertebrate Zoology with Invertebrate Zoology and Entomology, ... 1
(7) Botany and Geology, ... 1
(8) Architecture, ... 1
(9) Agriculture, Horticulture, and Veterinary Science, . 1
(10) English, ... 1
(11) Germanic Languages, ... 1
(12) Romance Languages, ... 1

(b) The ten graduate scholarships to the ten following departments and groups of departments:

(1) Mathematics, ... 1
(2) Chemistry, ... 1
(3) Physics, ... 1
(4) Civil Engineering, ... 1
(5) Mechanical and Electrical Engineering, ... 1
(6) Latin and Greek, ... 1
(7) Archæology and Comparative Philology, ... 1
(8) Physiology and Vertebrate Zoology with Invertebrate Zoology and Entomology, ... 1
(9) Botany and Geology, ... 1
(10) English, ... 1

At the meeting on May 11 a communication from the Executive Committee concerning the assignment of fellowships was presented, as follows:

36

The Executive Committee at its meeting on Tuesday, the 8th of May, took the following action :

"Moved and carried, that in reference to the communication from the General Faculty in regard to assignment of scholarships and fellowships, that one fellowship be reserved for the Law School, and that the General Faculty be requested to assign the fellowships and scholarships accordingly."

It was then moved and carried that the Committee on Scholarships be asked to report a scheme of readjustment.

Professor Crane from the committee then reported in a manner supplementary to their report of last week. This report was adopted and the previous report amended accordingly, as follows :

The Committee on Scholarships begs to present the following report supplementary to their report of May 4. Whereas, since the meeting of May 4th, the Executive Committee of the Trustees has transferred to the Law School one of the thirteen fellowships assigned in the report of May 4, and recommitted to the Committee the whole matter for readjustment, the Committee would recommend the [following changes in this report of May 4 :

1st, That for the assignment of fellowships and scholarships the departments of Germanic and Romance Languages constitute one group and receive one fellowship and one scholarship.

2d, That the scholarship assigned to Mechanical and Electrical Engineering (Sibley College) be withdrawn.

PADGHAM SCHOLARSHIP.

Records D, p. 161.

Voted that the rules which apply to the awarding of the general scholarships shall apply also to the Padgham Scholarship.

STANDING COMMITTEES OF THE FACULTY, 1894-5.

Records D, p. 161.

[For the origin and functions of the committees see pp. 27-28 of these reprints.]

Admission on Certificate.—The Dean, Professors Wilder, Oliver, Hart, Bennett.

Advanced Standing.—The Dean, the Registrar, Professors Prentiss, Crane, Fuertes, Williams, Thurston, Wait, Creighton.

Graduate Work and Advanced Degrees.—The Dean, Professors Caldwell, Fuertes, Comstock, Thurston, Wheeler, Jenks, Merritt, Wait.

Doubtful Cases.—The Dean, the Registrar, Professors Crane, Fuertes, Thurston, Hitchcock, Gage, Jones, Babcock.

Records of Candidates for Graduation.—The Dean, the Registrar, Professors Caldwell, Oliver, Fuertes, Thurston, Hart, Burr, Bennett.

Register and Announcement of Courses.—The President, the Dean, the Registrar.

Changes in Registration.—The Dean, the Secretary, and the Heads of Departments concerned.

Scholarships.—Professors Crane, Wilder, Hewett, Wheeler, Wait, Crandall, Ryan.

Military and Gymnasium.—The Dean, the Professor of Physical Culture, the Commandant.

Athletics.—Dr. Hitchcock, the Commandant, Professors White, Wheeler, Dennis.

Assignment of Freshmen.—Professor Jones, with the aid of Instructors to be designated.

Excusing Labor Students from Drill and Gymnasium.—Professors Comstock, Gage, Burr.

Leave of Absence.—The President, the Registrar.

Summer School.—Professors Bennett, Caldwell, Burr, Bailey, O. F. Emerson.

GRADUATE WORK.

Records D, p. 162.

Voted, 1. That the regular term records include a mention of the work and progress of graduate students in such form as may be convenient.

2. That at the end of the year the chairmen of all special committees having in charge the work of graduate students report to the chairman of the general committee regarding the amount and quality of such work.

DOCTORS' DEGREES.

Records D, p. 163.

Resolved, That the Committee on Graduate Work be requested to consider and report as to the advisability of more clearly defining the nature of the study leading to the degrees of Doctor of Philosophy and Doctor of Science, or of merging these degrees in one.

Records D, p. 164.

The Committee on Graduate Work reported the following resolution : That in the opinion of the Committee it would be inadvisable to alter the present requirements for the Doctors' degrees. The resolution was adopted.

38

Records D, p. 165.

Recommended by the Committee on Graduate Work :
That in the list of graduate students in the Register be printed (1)
the names of graduate students actually in residence or candidates *in
absentia*, or studying in absence by special permission of the Faculty
either at other universities or as holders of fellowships; and (2) in a
separate list, with the caption *graduate students not in residence for
1894-95*, the names of those students who have completed the mini-
mum of residence required, and who are reported by the special committees as continuing their work under direction with the intention of
coming up for examination.

WOODFORD PRIZE.

Records D, pp. 166, 167.

The following revised conditions respecting the Woodford Prize were
adopted.

The Woodford Prize founded by the Hon. Stewart Lyndon Woodford, and consisting of a gold medal of the value of one hundred dollars, will be given annually for the best English oration, both matter
and manner being taken into account.

The prize may be competed for under the following conditions :

1. Any member of the Senior class who is to receive a degree at the
coming Commencement, may be a competitor, provided he has taken
at least one course of instruction in Elocution and Oratory.

2. Every competitor shall be required to submit, at the Registrar's
office, on or before the first day of the Spring term, an original oration
upon a subject which shall have previously been approved by the Professor of Elocution and Oratory.

3. The competing orations shall be limited to fifteen hundred words
and shall be written with a typewriter.

4. The orations submitted shall be read in private by their authors
to a committee appointed by the Faculty, after which the committee
shall examine the orations and shall select the best, not to exceed six
in number, for delivery in public. The names of the successful writers
shall be announced as early as is practicable after the beginning of the
Spring Term.

5. The contest for the prize will take place on the evening of the
fifth Friday of the Spring Term, under the direction of the President
of the University.

6. The prize shall be awarded by a committee of three to be appointed by the President and, whenever practicable, from persons not
resident in Ithaca.

39

7. The prize shall not be conferred unless the successful competitor shall complete the course and take the degree at the Commencement next following.

8. A copy of each of the orations selected for the competition shall, within one week after the selection, be deposited by its author with the committee charged with the selection, who shall, after the completion of the competition, deposit the orations permanently in the University Library.

UNIVERSITY CALENDAR.

Records D, p. 167.

On motion the following dates were fixed in the University calendar :

1. The evening of the day preceding Founder's Day, or as near this date as may be possible—'94 Memorial Prize Debate.

2. The first day of the Spring Term—the latest date for presenting Woodford Orations.

3. The second Friday in May—the latest date for presenting Commencement Orations.

4. The fourth Friday preceding Commencement—'86 Memorial Prize Competition.

DEATH OF HERBERT TUTTLE.

Records D, pp. 168, 169.

On the morning of Commencement Day, June the 21st, 1894, there passed from earth our colleague, Professor Herbert Tuttle. In resuming without him the duties in which he was so long our associate, it is fitting that we put upon record our deep sense of his worth and of our loss.

From his entrance into this Faculty in the autumn of 1881, Professor Tuttle took an active and efficient part in the conduct of the University. The keenness of his mind, the vigor and courage of his convictions, his invincible independence, his experience of affairs, his power of exact and cogent statement, gave at all times weight to his counsels. To the work of his class-room he brought the same wealth of research, the same maturity of judgment, the same precision of diction, the same grace of literary expression, which give just eminence to his published writings. In all his University relations, the uncompromising honesty of his nature, impatient of pretense and equivocation, his humor, keen and often caustic, his sensitive and agressive temper, his outrightness and downrightness, stamped with the force of a positive individuality whatever he said or did. By all who knew him well and not least by his colleagues in this Faculty, he must ever be sorely missed and sincerely mourned.

40

The Committee recommends that this expression of our grief be made a part of the records of the Faculty and communicated to the relatives of our late colleague.

SCHOLARSHIP EXAMINATIONS.

Records D, p. 169.

Moved and carried, that the date of the Scholarship examinations be placed as soon after the entrance examinations as possible.

REGISTRATION CARDS.

Records D, p. 170.

The request of the Registrar to be allowed to accept delayed registration cards without requiring each student to petition the Faculty was granted.

DOUBTFUL CASES.

Records D, p. 171.

Moved and carried, that all matters pertaining to dropped students be referred to the Doubtful Case Committee with power. [Cp. Records D, p. 86.]

ATHLETICS.

Records D, p. 175.

Moved and carried, that the Faculty deems it advisable to limit intercollegiate football contests, so far as feasible, to college grounds, and is of the opinion that no student who is markedly deficient in his University work should be allowed to play on the team. It believes further that the number of absences from town should be reduced, and would reiterate its resolution of Oct. 5th, 1894, viz. : "We do not regard any person as qualified to be a member of a University team who comes to the University without the intention of remaining at least one year, or who receives any remuneration or consideration of any sort for his services."

Records D, p. 177.

The following resolution was presented, and after discussion, failed of adoption :

Resolved, That the Committee on Athletics is hereby directed not to grant leaves of absence to students or teams for the purpose of playing baseball with other than college teams.

41

EXAMINATIONS.

Records D, p. 177.

Moved and carried, that beginning with the Spring Term the Faculty will return to the old system of reserving a space of time at the end of each term for examinations, with the understanding that the space be made as small as possible, that the larger examinations be placed as late as possible, and that each professor under the general rule of the Faculty (ch. IV, pp. 6, 21 of Reprints,) be at liberty either to apply for a reserved space or to examine as heretofore during the hours of recitation.

REQUIREMENTS IN ARTS AND PHILOSOPHY.

Records D, p. 178.

Resolved, That in the next issue of the Register, the requirements for admission to the courses in Arts and in Philosophy be amended by the substitution on page 33 for the words " Fyffe's Primer of Greece " and " Creighton's Primer of Rome" of the words " Myers' History of Greece and Allen's History of Rome," and that in and after the year 1896–97 the number of hours required of Freshmen in the courses in Arts and Philosophy be reduced by the omission of the two hours now assigned to Grecian and Roman History, this reduced number of hours to be made the maximum for Freshmen in these courses.

Further change was made in the course of study in Arts by requiring the election in the Sophomore year of at least two hours in the courses of the School of History and Political Science. The two hours, which must now be elected in History in the Sophomore year in the course in Philosophy may be taken in either History or Political Science.

GENERAL LEGISLATION OF THE FACULTY AND EXTRACTS FROM THE FACULTY RECORDS.

APRIL 19, 1895—JUNE 18, 1895.

RESOLUTIONS ON THE DEATH OF PROFESSOR OLIVER.

Records D, p. 180.

The Faculty of Cornell University, desiring to show their appreciation of the character and services of their late colleague, Professor Oliver, have directed that the following expression of their sorrow and sympathy be incorporated in their records, and be communicated to the family of their departed associate.

In the death of James Edward Oliver this Faculty mourn the loss of a colleague endeared to them through many years of intimate association, by his warm friendliness, his frank and gentle nature, his patient conscientiousness, and his steadfast adherence to high standards of thought and conduct.

In him the body of students have lost a faithful and inspiring teacher, and a devoted friend; and the cause of education is deprived of a liberal and earnest advocate, and a thinker original and profound.

His memory will always be cherished as one who long bore a prominent part in the development of the University, and contributed greatly in matters of scholarship and administration to its progress and success.

SUMMER SCHOOL.

Records D, p. 183.

The Committee on the Summer School recommend that hereafter University students in the Summer School shall have the privilege of taking an examination at the termination of the Summer session in any subject pursued in the school in which the instructor is willing to give one, the mark for such examination to be subject to the approval of the head of the department in which the work is taken. [This resolution was lost.]

ADVANCED DEGREES IN ABSENTIA.

Records D, p. 185.

The Committee appointed to consider the desirability of continuing the practice of conferring degrees *in absentia* made the following report, which was adopted:

42

43

The committee see no reason for any change of the present rules, except by making them more specific, so as to accord with actual practice in administering them, by providing *first*, that each candidate shall pursue a course of study prescribed by the appropriate committee : *second*, that he shall appear in person at the University for examinations, and to receive his diploma at Commencement.

SECRETARYSHIP OF THE FACULTY.

Records D, p. 186.

The resignation of Professor George P. Bristol as secretary was accepted and Professor W. F. Willcox was elected in his stead.

The resignation of Professor L M. Dennis as Assistant-Secretary was accepted.

COMMUNICATION SIGNED BY 649 STUDENTS.

Records D, p. 186.

To the President and Members of the Faculty :

We, the undersigned, students of Cornell University, accept the recent action of the Faculty in regard to University athletics as an expression of confidence in the system recently introduced for the government of the University as a whole and of its athletics, and as an expression also of satisfaction with the workings of the systems. We are sensible of the trust reposed in us, as indicated by this refusal to introduce, by interference with the regular governing bodies, an element of paternalism into the government of the students, and of their athletic interests. We, therefore, wish to renew our pledge that, as long as this trust remains upon us, we shall do everything in our power to prevent anything which might in any way bring discredit upon the University.

REPORTS ON SENIOR WORK.

Records D, p. 188.

Resolved : That in the judgment of the Faculty it is necessary and that it therefore be required that hereafter all senior work be reported to the Registrar not later than six P. M. on the Saturday preceding Commencement.

Furthermore that the Registrar furnish upon application a list of candidates for graduation to professors desiring the same.

ASSISTANT SECRETARYSHIP.

Records D, p. 188.

Mr. D. F. Hoy was elected Assistant-Secretary of the Faculty.

GENERAL LEGISLATION OF THE FACULTY AND EXTRACTS FROM THE FACULTY RECORDS.

SEPT. 27, 1895—APRIL 10, 1896.

SPECIAL STUDENTS.

Records E, p. 9, October 11, 1895.

Persons at least twenty-one years of age may be admitted as special students, without examination, provided they give evidence of ability to do creditably special work in the University, are recommended to the Faculty by the professor in charge of the department of study in which they desire to take a large part of their work, and have not already been admitted to the University, nor, having applied for admission, have been rejected. By direction of the Faculty the recommendation of a special student is to be referred to a committee for provisional acceptance, before final ratification by the Faculty. Candidates for admission as special students should correspond directly with the professor in whose department they expect to take work, in order to secure such recommendation. Such students may graduate in any of the courses, on condition of passing all the required examinations, including those for admission. Students are not permitted to make up deficiencies in entrance subjects by attending university instruction in those subjects, but are required to take the necessary instruction outside of the University. Special students are subject to the same regulations in regard to examinations and number of hours as students in the general courses.

DEGREES IN ABSENTIA—(COMMUNICATION FROM THE EXECUTIVE COMMITTEE).

Records E, p. 11, October 18, 1895.

Resolved, That the Faculty be requested to consider the wisdom of continuing the policy of granting degrees to graduate students *in absentia*, and to report recommendations to the Board of Trustees.

DEGREES IN ABSENTIA.

Records p. 13, October 18, 1895.

Resolved, That residence at the University is required for all degrees except that in special cases graduates of this University, on the recommendation of the special committee that would have charge of their work, may, by vote of the Faculty in each case, become candi-

44

dates for the degrees of M.C.E., M.M.E., and M.S. in Agr., after two years of professional practice and study *in absentia*.

STANDING COMMITTEES OF THE FACULTY, 1895-96.

Records E, p. 12, October 18, 1895.

The following list of standing committees of the Faculty for the year 1895–96 was reported by the President :

Admission on Certificate.—The Dean, Professors Wilder, McMahon, Hart, Bristol.

Advanced Standing.—The Dean, the Registrar, Professors Prentiss, Crane, Fuertes, S. G. Williams, Thurston, Wait, Creighton..

Graduate Work and Advanced Degrees.—The Dean, Professors Caldwell, Fuertes, Comstock, Thurston, Bennett, Morse Stephens, Nichols, Wait.

Doubtful Cases.—The Dean, the Registrar, Professors Crane, Fuertes, Thurston, Bennett, Hitchcock, Gage, Jones, Babcock.

Records of Candidates for Graduation.—The Dean, the Registrar, Professors Caldwell, Jones, Fuertes, Thurston, Hart, Burr, Bennett.

Register and Announcement of Courses.—The President, the Dean, the Registrar.

Changes in Registration.—The Dean, the Assistant Secretary, and the Heads of Departments concerned.

Scholarships.—Professors Crane, Hewett, Bristol, Wait, Crandall, Ryan.

Military and Gymnasium.—The Dean, the Professor of Physical Culture, the Commandant.

Athletics.—Dr. Hitchcock, the Commandant, Professors White, Merritt, Dennis.

Assignment of Freshmen.—Professor Jones, with the aid of Instructors to be designated.

Excusing Labor Students from Drill and Gymnasium.—Professors Comstock, Gage, Burr.

Leave of Absence.—The President, the Registrar.

Summer School.—Professors Bennett, Caldwell, Burr, Bailey, O. F. Emerson.

SUMMER SCHOOL.

Records E, p. 14, October 25, 1895.

From the Committee on Summer School, the announcement of courses to be offered next summer was received, and after discussion they were referred to the Committee on University Publications, with power.

46

ENGLISH IN EXAMINATION PAPERS.

Records E, p. 15, October 25, 1895.

Desiring that all the Departments in the University may coöperate with the English Department in its efforts to raise the standard, the Faculty make the following recommendations :

1. That every examiner consider himself warranted in conditioning or rejecting any paper which contains bad spelling or other gross faults of expression, or in which technical terms are used incorrectly.

2. That examination papers be returned to the writers, mistakes in English being underscored or in some other way made plain to the eye.

COLLEGE ENTRANCE REQUIREMENTS.

Records E, p. 17, November 8, 1895.

Resolved, That this Faculty indicate to President Low its readiness to coöperate with Columbia in the proposition to secure uniform entrance requirements to colleges.

CALENDAR. TUITION FEE FOR GRADUATE STUDENTS. (COMMUNICATION FROM THE BOARD OF TRUSTEES.)

Records E, p. 20, November 15, 1895.

The Board of Trustees at its meeting on the 13th, took action as follows :

Moved and carried, that the action of the Executive Committee of December 12th, 1893, accepting and adopting the recommendations of the Faculty contained in communication of that date, be repealed.

Moved and carried, that the Board of Trustees adopt the existing University Calendar, so far as concerns term time and holidays, subject to the right of any faculty to suspend University exercises of which it has charge, for one day on special occasions.

Moved and carried, that hereafter graduate students studying for a degree "in absentia" be charged one year's tuition, in the department in which they are studying, payable in advance.

Yours truly,
(Signed) E. L. WILLIAMS, Sec'y.

From the minutes.

ELECTIVE WORK IN GENERAL·COURSES.

Records E, p. 21, November 15, 1895.

Resolved, That the following action of the Faculty be repealed :
(cf. Records D, p. 137, March 19, 1894.)

47

2. For the degree of Bachelor of Science the majority of the elective work shall be in Natural Science or Mathematics, beginning with the class graduating in 1896. 6. In the courses in Arts and Philosophy, the major part of the elective work shall be in literary, historical, philosophical, or mathematical subjects. But this resolution shall not affect the existing regulations in regard to electing studies in the School of Law.

COMMITTEE ON ENTRANCE REQUIREMENTS, COURSES, AND DEGREES.

Records E, pp. 23-24, November 22, 1895.

Resolved, That a committee of nine be appointed by the President to consider and report upon the feasibility :

1. Of establishing a general system of entrance requirements similar in the main to those for the present course in Philosophy, and applicable to all non-technical students ;

2. Of conferring one general degree, namely, Bachelor of Arts ;

3. Of establishing lines of study in Science and in Letters in place of the present system of general courses.

CALENDAR.

Records E, p. 24, November 22, 1895.

The question of arranging the calendar with reference to the Christmas recess in 1896 was referred to the President and Dean with power.

ALUMNÆ SCHOLARSHIP.

Records E, p. 25, December 6, 1895.

From the Board of Trustees the following communication was read :

"The Board of Trustees at its meeting on the 13th, accepted from the Associate Alumnæ an undergraduate scholarship of $100 for the present University year, and a like sum for each year hereafter so long as the sum is raised by annual subscription. The scholarship is to be given under the following conditions :

(a) It shall be awarded to a self-supporting woman who has already spent at least one year in the University as a student.

(b) The basis of award shall be excellence of scholarship as shown by the University records and a need of financial aid.

(c) The nomination for the scholarship shall be made by a committee of the Alumnæ, who, after consultation with the Dean of the General Faculty and the Registrar as to the standing of the applicants, shall decide as to which one of them will be most benefitted by the financial aid of the scholarship.

(d) The approval of said nomination by the President of the University shall constitute an appointment."

COURSES IN MUSIC.

Records E, p. 26, December 6, 1895.

The special order was then taken up and after discussion it was voted that one hour's credit per week be allowed to students in the University who successfully complete either of the two courses of instruction controlled by the Executive Committee of the Choral Union, namely\: 1. A course in anthem singing and hymnology, one and one-half hours per week ; 2. A course in elementary sight reading, one and one-half hours per week. Only those students being eligible for credit who present to the Registrar at the end of each term a statement countersigned by the Chairman of the Executive Committee, to the effect that their work has been thorough and their progress satisfactory.

DRILL AND GYMNASIUM.

Records E, p. 27, December 6, 1895.

A student deficient in a term of Military Drill or Gymnastics is not permitted to substitute anything else for that work, or to be excused from any subsequent term until the deficiency is removed.

COMMENCEMENT PROGRAMME.

Records E, p. 28, December 13, 1895.

On the motion of the Professor of German a special committee of five, with the President as chairman, was created to consider the improvement of the Commencement programme.

EXAMINATIONS.

Records E, p. 28, December 13, 1895.

Resolved, That, in case of an actual conflict of examination assignments, any professor may arrange for a special examination upon informing the Registrar of the intended action. Carried.

ENTRANCE REQUIREMENTS.

Records E, p. 31, January 10, 1896.

WHEREAS : The present requirements for admission to the professional and scientific courses are unequal, in such a manner that they entail hardships to the instructing officers, damage to the students, and unnecessary expenses to the University, and

49

WHEREAS, The entire question of entrance conditions to these courses can be largely improved by a careful study of its details in order to overcome the above mentioned inconveniences, and add to the efficiency of the courses affected, whilst improving the preparation of candidates for admission ; therefore,

Resolved, That a committee be appointed by the President, consisting of two members of the Faculty from each of the said professional scientific schools, including the College of Agriculture, and two professors from the Faculty at large, who, under the chairmanship of the President of the Univsrsity, and either working as a whole, or by sub-committees, be required to study the bearing of this question, and finally prepare a report to the Faculty for its discussion, and such action as may be deemed wise and proper in these premises.

ENTRANCE ENGLISH IN REGENTS' DIPLOMAS.

Records E, p. 31, January 10, 1896.

Resolved, That candidates for admission presenting Regents' diplomas, shall not be exempt from the entrance examination in English unless they offer three full years of Regents' English, or eight Academic English counts (including English Composition, Higher English, and English Reading). This resolution shall go into effect in June, 1897.

MARKING SYSTEM.

Records E, pp. 34, 37, and 39, January 17, 1896.

Moved : That the present system of reporting the standing of students on the scale of 100 be abandoned, and that in its place only four grades be reported, namely, dropped, conditioned, passed, and excellent, each grade to be represented by a suitable letter.

Moved : That five grades be recognized.

Moved : 1. That the percentage system of grading students in the general courses be abandoned.

2. That the standing of students (in the general courses) be indicated by the terms : passed, conditioned, failed.

3. That in the form for reports a column be reserved for remarks by the professor.

After discussion the whole subject was laid upon the table.

ENTRANCE CONDITIONS.

Records E, p. 39, February 7, 1896.

Resolved, That a student against whom there is a condition upon an entrance requirement, be not allowed to register for a second year's study without permission of the Faculty.

50

LIBRARY BULLETIN.

Records E, p. 40, February 21, 1896.

A communication from the University Librarian with reference to the expediency of continuing the publication of the University Bulletin was read, and after discussion it was voted that the Library Council be requested to consider the possibility of publishing in the place of the present Library Bulletin a brief list of the accessions to the University Library at frequent intervals.

UNIVERSITY SCHOLARSHIP EXAMINATIONS.

Records E, p. 41, February 21, 1896.

Resolved, That it is inexpedient to admit to the scholarship examinations any one who has not fully completed the specific entrance requirements of his course.

COMMITTEE ON ENTRANCE REQUIREMENTS, COURSES, AND DEGREES.

Records E, p. 42, March 6, 1896.

The report of the Committee appointed November 22, 1895, was presented by its chairman as follows :

"The committee appointed in accordance with the resolution of November 22, 1895, to consider the questions of general entrance requirements, courses of study, and degrees, begs leave to report :

That in the opinion of this Committee it is not desirable to establish a general system of entrance requirements, similar to those for the present course in Philosophy, and applicable to all non-technical students.

And to recommend :

1. That candidates for admission to non-technical study be permitted to elect between the groups of advanced requirements established for 1897 in Arts, Philosophy, and Science, as indicated at pp. 33–35 of the Register for 1895–96, namely :

a. Greek and Latin.

b. Latin, and two years of either French of German.

c. Two years of French, two years of German, and one year of advanced Mathematics (*i. e.*, Solid Geometry, Advanced Algebra, Plane Trigonometry).

2. That after admission the following subjects (only) be required of them for the baccalaureate degree :

a. One year of English, five hours a week, in the Freshman year (instead of the present three hours in the Freshman and two hours in the Sophomore year).

b. Military Drill, Gymnasium, and Thesis, as at present (Drill and Gymnasium to be included in the 180 hours required for graduation).

3. That in all other respects they have freedom of election under the limitations to be prescribed by each department.

Students to be advised and encouraged, but not required, to lay out definite or systematic lines of study.

4. That the single degree of Bachelor of 'Arts be conferred, irrespective of the studies elected.

> J. M. HART, Chairman,
> G. L. BURR,
> T. F. CRANE,
> E. L. NICHOLS,
> L. A. WAIT,
> H. S. WHITE,
> B. G. WILDER,
> S. G. WILLIAMS."

The undersigned, a minority of the Committee appointed to report on the advisability of changing the present basis of granting the A.B. degree, begs leave to recommend that no change be made at present in the basis of granting the A.B. degree.

> (Signed) C. E. BENNETT.

RESIGNATION OF PROFESSOR PRENTISS.

Records E, p. 46, March 20, 1896.

The report of the Committee appointed to draft resolutions regarding the resignation of the Professor of Botany was presented and ordered to be spread upon the minutes, as follows:

WHEREAS, The President of the University has informed the Faculty that Professor Albert N. Prentiss has resigned the chair of botany, which he has filled since the earliest days of this University, and that the Trustees have accepted the said resignation with regret at the continued ill health that finally decided Professor Prentiss to take this step, and

WHEREAS, The terms under which the resignation was accepted evince the appreciation of the Trustees for the services rendered by Professor Prentiss, whom they have honored by an election as Emeritus Professor, among other proofs of their esteem ; and

WHEREAS, The separation of Professor Prentiss from active connection with the Faculty, in which his presence and labors have been so often of signal value to the cause of education and of advantage to the interests and progress of the University, calls for a suitable expression of the feelings of the Faculty at this moment; therefore,

Resolved, That the Faculty of Cornell University will ever bear in its recollection the long and useful services of our colleague, and will

ever remember the important role he took in its counsels; his honest and effective service and uncompromising loyalty to the interests of truth, and especially the important help he contributed to the establishment of the ideals upon which this University was founded, in the early days when all the courage and faith of its professors was fully tested by the new problems that this institution had to solve in the face of universal opposition, guided by no precedents and depending only upon the sturdy, strong conviction of the band of pioneers who, without experience and under discouraging difficulties, laid the foundations of our present prosperity and eminence in the educational fields of our country.

It is proper that Professor Prentiss should be distinguished by his peers and the successors of the original Faculty of Cornell University by this tribute to his sterling virtues as a gentleman, colleague, and pioneer; and be it further

Resolved, That, with our sincere prayer for the restoration of his health, the foregoing statements be spread upon the minutes of this Faculty as part of the history of its transactions, a copy of them be sent to Professor Prentiss as a token of our friendship and to the Trustees and the press as a proof of our appreciation of the long and useful services of our retiring colleague.

E. A. FUERTES,

G. C. CALDWELL,

T. F. CRANE,

Committee.

Records E, p. 49, April 10, 1896.

The following communication from the Professor Emeritus of Botany was read and ordered spread upon the minutes.

CORNELL UNIVERSITY, April 9, 1896.

Professor W. F. Willcox,

Secretary of the Faculty,

DEAR SIR:

Your favor of March 21 enclosing a copy of resolutions passed by the Faculty regarding my resignation of the Professorship of Botany, has been duly received. May I ask you to communicate to my honored colleagues the very high value in which I hold their kindly sympathy and words of approval expressed in the action to which this note refers.

Sincerely yours,

(Signed)   ALBERT N. PRENTISS.

CALENDAR.

Records E, p. 50, April 10, 1896.

The question of arranging the calendar of the University in order to enable the Faculty of the Law School to adjust their dates in harmony with it, was referred to the President and Dean with power.

GENERAL LEGISLATION OF THE FACULTY AND EXTRACTS FROM THE FACULTY RECORDS.

APRIL 17, 1896—JUNE 16, 1896.

COMMENCEMENT EXERCISES.

Records E, p. 52, April 17, 1896.

Resolved, That for the present year the rules regulating Commencement stage orations be suspended, and that the matter of Commencement exercises be referred to the President with power.

REORGANIZATION OF THE FACULTIES OF THE UNIVERSITY.

Records E, p. 52, April 17, 1896.

The following resolutions of the Executive Committee were presented by the President:

"*Resolved,* That a committee be appointed to devise and report a scheme for the reorganization of the Faculties of the University, having regard to both those now in existence and those which may hereafter be added, with a view, on the one hand, to securing and safeguarding the unity of the educational forces of the University, and on the other, of differentiating them so as to produce the maximum of efficiency,—the said committee being, however, instructed, while providing for a different combination and distribution, to make no change by way of increase or diminution, in the entirety of the functions now exercised by the Faculties. For the better discharge of this work the committee is also instructed to confer with a committee of the General Faculty and a committee of the Faculty of the Law School.

Further *Resolved,* That the President be authorized to communicate this resolution to the aforesaid Faculties, with the request that committees of conference be appointed, and to arrange the date and place of the first meeting."

And it was voted that a committee of eleven be appointed by the President as a committee of the General Faculty to confer with the other committees. The following names were subsequently reported by the President as constituting that committee: The Dean, Professors Roberts, Babcock, Fuertes, Thurston, Caldwell, Nichols, Comstock, M. C. Tyler, Crane, Wait.

53

54

ENTRANCE EXAMINATIONS FOR LAW STUDENTS.

Records E, p. 53, April 17, 1896.

"*Resolved,* That those departments conducting entrance examinations which may find it convenient, be authorized to admit to such examinations applicants for admission to the School of Law."

ENTRANCE REQUIREMENTS FOR THE COLLEGE OF CIVIL ENGINEERING.

Records E, p. 53, April 17, 1896.

The Director of the College of Civil Engineering moved that in and after June, 1898, the entrance requirements for the College of Civil Engineering be made to conform to the entrance requirements for the other technical scientific schools, namely, that advanced algebra and plane and spherical trigonometry be added to those requirements ; and the resolution was carried.

ELECTIVE WORK IN GENERAL COURSES.

Records E, p. 59, May 8, 1896.

The Registrar raised the question whether the repeal of Sections 2 and 6 in the requirements for admission and degrees, which was voted November 22, 1895, (see Reprints, p. 47) went into effect at once, and it was ruled that it did.

REGENTS' EXAMINATIONS.

Records E, p. 60, May 8, 1896.

The petition of a student for credit on a Regents pass in Cæsar, obtained after entrance to the University and offered in place of the entrance examination required, was refused.

MODERN LANGUAGE REQUIREMENT FOR THE COURSE IN SCIENCE.

Records E, p. 61, May 8, 1896.

Resolved, That the alternate requirement of French and German for the third year in Science be eliminated.

ENTRANCE REQUIREMENTS, COURSES, AND DEGREES.

Records E, pp. 62, 68, 70, 74, May 15, 22, 29.

(Cf. Reprints, pp. 47, 50-51.)

Resolved, 1. That candidates for admission to non-technical study be permitted to elect between the groups of advanced requirements established for 1897 in Arts, Philosophy, and Science, as indicated at pages 33-35 of the Register of 1895-96, namely :

a. Greek and Latin.

b. Latin, and the advanced requirement in either French or German.

c. The advanced requirement in French, the advanced requirement in German, and one year of advanced mathematics, (*i. e.*, Solid Geometry, Advanced Algebra, Plane and Sperical Trigonometry).

2. That after admission the following subjects be required for the baccalaureate degree, namely :

Military Drill, Gymnasium, and Thesis, as at present ; but that in the cases of students not taking Drill and Gymnasium, an equivalent in hours be added to the 180 hours required for graduation.

3. That in all other respects they have freedom of election under the limitations to be prescribed by each department. Students to be advised and encouraged, but not required, to lay out definite or systematic lines of study.

4. That the single degree of Bachelor of Arts be conferred, irrespective of the studies elected.

The foregoing legislation is to go into effect with the class entering in 1897.

SCHOLARSHIP EXAMINATIONS.

Records E, p. 66, May 22, 1896.

The Committee on Scholarships reported a recommendation which was adopted, namely : That the following amendment be inserted in the Register on page 168, after 5 (f) German :

"The above examinations cover substantially the same ground as the entrance examinations in the respective subjects, except that the amount of French and German is that required for admission to the courses in engineering and architecture."

REORGANIZATION OF THE FACULTIES OF THE UNIVERSITY.

Records E, p. 71, May 29, 1896.

The following statute for the reorganization of the faculties of Cornell University was reported from the Executive Committee of the Board of Trustees, as having been enacted May 26, 1896, and it was ordered to be spread upon the minutes :

"1. *The University.*—Cornell University comprehends the following departments, to-wit : The Graduate Department, the Academic Department (or Department of Arts and Sciences), the College of Law, the College of Civil Engineering, the Sibley College of Mechanical Engineering and Mechanic Arts, the College of Architecture, and

the College of Agriculture. The New York State Veterinary College is administered by Cornell University, and its work is organically connected with that of the University.

"2 *The Faculties.*—The Faculties of Cornell University are :

(A) A General Faculty, designated THE UNIVERSITY FACULTY ; and (B) Special Faculties as follows :

1. THE FACULTY OF ARTS AND SCIENCES.
2. THE FACULTY OF LAW.
3. THE FACULTY OF CIVIL ENGINEERING.
4. THE FACULTY OF MECHANICAL ENGINEERING.
5. THE FACULTY OF ARCHITECTURE.
6. THE FACULTY OF AGRICULTURE.
7. THE FACULTY OF VETERINARY MEDICINE.

"3. *The University Faculty.*—The University Faculty consists of the President, who is *ex-officio*, the presiding officer, and the Professors and Assistant Professors of the University, including the Professors and Assistant Professors of the New York State Veterinary College. It is the function of the University Faculty to consider questions which concern more than one Special Faculty, and questions of University policy. The Graduate Department is under the immediate charge of the University Faculty.

"4. *The Special Faculties.*—Each Special Faculty is composed of the President, who is *ex-officio* the presiding officer, and all Professors, Assistant Professors, and Instructors who teach in the department or departments under the charge of that Faculty, but Instructors shall not have the right to vote. Subject to the right of revision by the University Faculty on all matters affecting general University policy, it is the duty of each Special Faculty to determine the entrance requirements for its own students ; to prescribe and define courses of study for them ; to determine the requirements for such degrees as are offered to students under its jurisdiction ; to enact and enforce rules for the guidance and government of its students ; and to recommend to the Trustees such candidates for degrees as may have completed the requirements.

"5. *Directors and Deans.*—Every College has a Director and every Faculty has a Dean. The powers and functions of Directors are fixed at the time of their appointment. Directors are also Deans of their respective Faculties. The Dean of the University Faculty and the Dean of the Faculty of Arts and Sciences are each appointed by the Board of Trustees on the nomination of the President and with the concurrence of his Faculty. It is the function of the Dean to preside at the meetings of his Faculty in the absence of the President ; to receive and act upon such applications of students as may be referred to him by his Faculty ; to prepare and conduct the business of the sev-

eral committees of which he may be made by his Faculty the chairman ; and, in general, except as otherwise provided, to act as the executive officer of his Faculty.

"Enacted to take effect upon the day following next Commencement.—E. L. WILLIAMS, Secretary."

ENGLISH IN DIPLOMAS, ETC.

Records E, p. 74, May 29, 1896.

The Professor of Romance Languages, on behalf of the Professor of Latin, moved that in future English be the language employed in all diplomas granted by this University, and that the President in conferring degrees be requested to employ English only, and the motion was adopted.

FRESHMAN ELECTIVES.

Records E, p. 74, May 29, 1896.

Resolved : 1. That the Dean and Registrar, after consultation with the members of the Faculty in charge of the general courses, make an official list of the courses of study open for election by Freshmen.

2. That such list be published in the Register in connection with the announcement of the complete elective system.

3. That this list be accompanied by a statement that Freshmen may register for no courses not named in this list until the written consent of the professor in charge of the courses desired be presented to the Registrar.

ENTRANCE REQUIREMENTS TO THE COURSE IN AGRICULTURE.

Records E, p. 77, June 5, 1896.

The Professor of Agriculture moved that in and after 1898 the advanced entrance requirements to the Course in Agriculture be the same as those to the Course in Science in 1897, that is, advanced French, advanced German, and advanced mathematics (solid geometry, advanced algebra, and plane and spherical trigonometry). Carried.

ENGLISH IN THE COURSE IN ARCHITECTURE.

Records E, p. 77, June 5, 1896.

The Professor of Architecture moved that the subject of English be stricken out of the Course in Architecture for the freshman year, and the motion was carried.

58

CREDIT FOR WORK IN SUMMER SCHOOL.

Records E, p. 78, June 5, 1896.

Resolved, That university students 'doing work in the University Summer School may receive credit for ten hours of such work on passing the regular university examinations in the subjects so taken.

REPORT OF THE MEMBERS OF THE CONFERENCES ON UNIFORM COL-LEGE ENTRANCE REQUIREMENTS, AT WHICH REPRESENTATIVES FROM COLUMBIA, CORNELL, HARVARD, PENNSYLVANIA, PRINCE-TON, YALE, AND AN EQUAL NUMBER OF SECONDARY-SCHOOL TEACHERS WERE PRESENT.

Records E, p. 79, June 5, 1896.

It was reported that uniform college entrance requirements had been agreed upon in the subjects of Greek, Latin, Mathematics, French, German, and History, and that these requirements were sub-stantially the same as the present requirements at Cornell with the exception of Mathematics and History.

In Mathematics a slight addition was to be made to the amount of algebra, and arithmetic as a separate subject was to be discontinued. It was voted that these changes in Mathematics go into effect in and after 1897.

In History it was reported that the conference had decided to recom-mend an option between English, American, Grecian, and Roman History, and that the candidates must present two of the four sub-jects. It was resolved that this requirement go into effect at Cornell in and after 1898. It was then resolved that the Committee on Publi-cations be authorized to publish in the forthcoming Register the recommendations made by the various conferences.

Absences, III.
Adams. Resolutions adopted on retirement of President, 17.
Admission and degrees. Requirements for, 30.
Admission by certificate. Committee on, 10.
Admission. Arts and Philosophy, 41. Credentials of applicants for, 23. To Course in Letters, Latin for, 16. To Courses in Letters and Science, Latin for, 12.
Agriculture. Tuition, 3. Course in, 18. Entrance requirements to the Course in, 57.
Alumnæ Scholarship, 47.
Alumni, VIII.
Architecture. Entrance, Latin in, 25. English in, Course in, 57.
Arts. Course in, VII.
Arts and Philosophy. Requirements in, 41.
Athletics, General policy, V, 40. Standing committee on, 8. Athletic organizations, petitions from, 23. Eligibility, rule on, 34.

Bulletin. Publications of, weekly, 7.

Calendar, 26, 39, 46, 47, 52.
Certificates, VII. Teacher's, 2. Entrance, English, 21.
Civil Engineering. Entrance requirements to college of, 54.
Class banquets, 7.
Codification of Faculty Records, 23, 28. Report of Dean on, 28.
Co-education, V.
Columbian Exposition, 7.
Commencement exercises, 53.
Commencement programme, 48.
Committees, (See Standing Committees), I. Committee on admission by certificate, 10.
Conference. Regarding uniform entrance requirements, 58.
Council, student, 22.
Course in Agriculture. Entrance requirements to, 57; special short, 18; in Architecture, English in, 57; in Arts, VII. Elective work in general, 46; in History, Letters, Science, Natural History, rules for students in, 7; in Letters and Science, Latin, for admission to 12; in Music, 48; in Science, modern language requirement in, 54.
Courses and degrees. Committee on, 47, 50. Entrance requirements to, 54.
Credit for work, 16.

Dean of the General Faculty, 18. Codification of faculty records, 23. Report of, on codification, 28. Office of, 29.
Degrees, VIII. Candidacy for, 4. Requirements for, 30. Diploma for Doctor's,

12. Examinations for advanced, 24. Graduate work, for Master's degree, counting towards Doctor's degree, 29. Graduate work, reports on, 37. Special distinctions, 31. Doctor's, 37. Master's, regulations for 2; of Master of Letters, 3; Master of Philosophy, 3; Doctor of Science, 4. Conditions for, 20. Amendment to rules for, 31. For members of the Faculty, 25. In absentia, communication from committee, 44. In absentia, advanced, 42.
Degrees and Courses, Committee on, 47, 50. Entrance requirements, 54.
Discipline, VI. Standing committee on, 10. Student committee on, 31, 33.
Distinctions, special, 31.
Doctors' degrees. See Degrees.
Doctor of Science, degree of. See degrees.
Doubtful cases, 28, 40.
Drill, V, 25. Exemption from, 4. Aliens and Military Science, 6.
Drill and Gymnasium, 48.

Elective work, 7, In general courses, 46, 54.
Electives, Freshmen, 57.
English, 10. Certificate for entrance, 21. Entrance requirements in, 23. Entrance, in Regents' diplomas, 49; in the Course in Architecture, 57; in diplomas, 57; in examination papers, 46.
Entrance English. Certificates for, 21; in Regents' diplomas, 49.
Entrance examinations, 10, 24. For Law students, 54.
Entrance. Latin, change in, 16.
Entrance conditions, 49. Requirements, 46, 48. Passing, 15. Courses in Mechanical and Electrical Engineering, 19. College of Civil Engineering, 54. Committee on, 47, 50. Course in Agriculture, 57. Course in Architecture, 19. Courses and degrees, 54; in English, 23. Uniform, 58.
Examinations, IV, 6, 26, 41, 48. For state Scholarships, 12; entrance, 10, 24; entrance, for Law students, 54. Regents, 54. Resolution of Ex. Com., 17. Rules governing the management of, 22. Scholarships, 40, 55. Students failing in, 6, 16. University Scholarship, 50. Exam. books, official, 16.

Faculties of the University. Reorganization of, 53, 55.
Fellowship. The President White, 32.
Fellowships and Scholarships, 35.
Freshmen, electives, 57.

Graduate students, 46. Committee on, 13.
In Register, names of, 38.
Graduate work and degrees. See Degrees. Degrees, 29.
Gymnasium and Drill, 48.

Heilman, Oren Gibson. Death of, 34.
History. Grecian and Roman, 17.

Laboring students, 10.
Latin. Change in entrance, 16. Entrance in Architecture, 25. For admission to Course in Letters, 16. For admission to Courses in Letters and Science, 12. Performances, credit for, 24.
Law. School of, 13. Work by undergraduates in, 8. Petitions, 34. Students, entrance examinations for, 54.
Letters and Science. Latin, for admission to, 12.
Library Bulletin, 50.

Marking system, 49. Determination of term standing, 21.
Master's degree. Regulations for. *See* Degrees.
Master of Letters. *See* Degrees.
Master of Philosophy. *See* Degrees.
Music. Courses in, 48.

Oliver. Resolutions on death of Professor, 42.

Philosophy and Arts. Requirements in, 41.
Prentiss. Resignation of Professor, 51.
Prize. Ninety-four Memorial, 33.
Procedure. Faculty procedure and rules, I.
Professors. Election of, 3.
Physical culture, 6. Training in freshman year, 20.

Records. Codification of, 23, 28.
Regents' diplomas. Entrance English, in, 49. Examinations, 54.
Registration, III. Cards, 40. Days, 10.
Registers. Addresses for, 29. Advertisements in, 26.
Reorganization of the Faculties of the University, 53, 55.
Reports of senior work, 43.
Rules. Faculty procedure and, I. Students not in University to leave town, 21. For students, revision of, 32. For Woodford Prize Competition, amendment to, 6.

Scholarships, VII, 10. Alumnæ, 47. The Padgham, 36.
Scholarship examinations, 40, 50, 55. For state Scholarships, 12.
Scholarships and Fellowships, 35.
Science. Modern language, requirements in course, 54.
Science and Letters. Latin, for admission to, 12.
Secretaryship of Faculty, 43. Assistant, 43.
Senate. The University, 5.
Shackford. Death of Professor, 11.
Societies, VI.
Special students, 44.
Standing committees. (*See* Committees), 1, 9. Appeals from in doubtful cases, 28.
Athletics, 8. Of the Faculty, 1892-93, 18; 1893-94, 27; 1894-95, 36; 1895-96, 45. On discipline, 10; on graduate students, 13; on graduate work, 24. Petitions to graduate in less than four years, 18. Substitution for required work, 34.
Student committee on discipline, 31, 33.
Student offenders, 30.
Student Council. Management of examinations, 22.
Students. *See* Rules.
Students. Communication signed by 649, 43. Special, 44.
Summer school, 19, 25, 42, 45. Credit for work in, 58. Resolution to establish, 20.
Summer courses of study, 13.

Teachers' Certificates, 2.
Technical studies, VII.
Thanksgiving, 26. Recess, 2.
Theses, 3. Extension of time on, 15, 22. For Doctors' degrees, form of, 20. Graduate, not to have been previously published, 31. Mention of, 16. Titles of commencement, 23. Undergraduate, 32.
Tuition, 3. Agriculture, 3.
Tuttle. Death of Professor Herbert, 39.

Uniform entrance requirements, 58.

Woodford oration. Fraud concerning, 15. Prize, 38. Competition, amendment to rules for, 6.